57 Ways
To Take Control Of
Your Time And Your Life

Jim Meisenheimer

A Helbern Book

Helbern
Published by the Helbern Group
Bradenton, FL, U.S.A.

Helbern Group, Registered Offices:
13506 Blythefield Terrace, Bradenton, FL 34202

First Helbern Printing, September 2003
10 9 8 7 6 5 4 321

Library of Congress Catalogue Card Number: 2003109134

ISBN: 0-9637479-4-0

This book is dedicated to my brother Ray and his fellow NYC (Rescue 3) firemen who gave their lives September 11, 2001:

Ray Meisenheimer
Chris Blackwell
Tom Foley
Tom Gambino
Brian Hickey
Don Regan
Gerry Schrang
Joe Spor

Also by Jim Meisenheimer

47 Ways To Sell Smarter

50 More Ways To Sell Smarter

*How To Double Your Sales
Without Quadrupling Your Effort*

*The 12 Best Questions
To Ask Customers*

*How To Get Surefire Selling Results
During Tough Times (Audio)*

57 Ways To Take Control Of Your Time And Your Life

Contents

Part I

Managing Yourself

Part II

Managing Your Business

Part III

Managing How You Sell

Part IV

Managing The Miscellaneous

Part I

Managing Yourself

1 - Time Is Money

No one has enough time and yet everyone has all that there is. The phone just rang. A telephone salesperson wanted to sell me a subscription to the Libertyville Review, a local newspaper, for only $12.95. I explained that we already get two newspapers delivered, and I barely have time to read them. She ended the call by saying, "Thank you for your time."

Forget about time management. You can't manage time, but you can manage yourself. Here's some old advice that gets better with age.

1. Begin every day with a list of things to do in writing.
2. Add the names and phone numbers of people you must call.
3. Using numbers prioritize every item on your list.
4. If your list is long start with a six-pack. Prioritize the six most important items on your list.

If you struggle with how to prioritize your "To Do" list on a daily basis you're not alone. In the seminars and

Jim Meisenheimer

workshops I teach only 1 in 81 of the salespeople surveyed follow the above steps. Don't make prioritizing optional - make it a daily habit. Here are several ideas on how to separate what's important from what's not.

Gotta Do - These are high value, high content, and substantive things you must do. They are simply important and should be done promptly and enthusiastically. Putting these things off usually creates guilt. If you're feeling guilty a lot, now you know why.

Oughta Do - These things run a close second. They have value and are indeed important. Remember, they are in second place today. Tomorrow they may convert to a Gotta Do.

Betta Do - Yes, these things have a place on your list. Today however, they don't occupy the first six spots. Sometimes you put something on your list today to remind you, you Gotta Do it in 10 days. If your list were on a deck of cards, these items would be close to the bottom of the deck.

Nada Do - For some crazy and unknown reason you may have things on your list that add no value, have no substance, will never get done, will move from list to list, and just take up valuable list space. Let it go. Get a grip. Remove these items ASAP and lighten your load immediately.

I use my prioritized daily "To Do" list to navigate the days I work. I discovered the trip is always shorter and better when I use my M.A.P. (My Action Plan).

2

2 - Time Management – The Ultimate Oxymoron

It's not possible to manage time? You can't make the clock run faster? You can't make it run slower. You have no control over time. Each of us begins the day with 1,440 minutes. It's your personal inventory. You use the time or you lose the time. There are simply no alternatives. Each week has 168 hours, no more no less. While managing time is out, managing yourself is in. Remember, as Henry Ford once said, "Don't complain, don't explain."

Here are ten techniques for achieving more in less time.

1. Get up 30 minutes earlier every day. Do the math and see how much extra time it gives you over the span of one year.

2. Take a course in self-management or one in priority management.

3. Commit to keeping a time log for one entire week. Record every activity and the time you give it. Your time busters will become very apparent.

4. Throughout the day routinely and quietly ask yourself, "Am I making the very best use of my time right now?"

5. Never do a task if there is a more important one to be done. Never! Foregoing priorities gets you off track more than anything else.

6. Build flextime into every day's schedule to allow for the unexpected. To do this is wise, not to do this is foolhardy.

7. Buy a timer. Time all phone calls, meetings, and projects. There is nothing more precious than your time. Don't you squander it and don't permit others to steal your time.

8. Set aside one hour every week getting rid of things (personally and professionally) you don't need and can live with out. It's called simplifying. Most of us have too much stuff that we can live without.

9. Take a few moments to write your own epitaph. Really do it. After you write it, look at it, and ask yourself "Is this the life I'm leading?" It's never too late to make changes in your life. I take that back, it's probably too late when someone else starts writing your epitaph.

10. Learn to say NO! Try saying it firmly and softly at least once a day to any unreasonable requests.

There is a reason why you need more time. It's because you're attempting too much. Plan your life and plan your days. If you want more balance in your life . . . schedule it.

3 - Travel Tips For The Road Warrior

Here are seven ideas you can use to make road travel easier for yourself. These tips run the gamut from "the practical" to the "you gotta be kidding me." Hope your travel is safer and better in the future. Also, if you have any ideas you want to share, please send them to me at jim@meisenheimer.com.

1. For Pete's sake, you'd like some peace and quiet when you travel, especially on airplanes. Check out Sony's noise cancellation headphones (SONY.COM). Not only do they filter out undesirable noise, they'll make listening to your favorite CD even more enjoyable.

2. Divide your flying time into two distinct parts. Allocate a specific amount of time for work and a specific amount of time for pleasure, i.e. watching a movie, listening to a CD, or reading a novel. On the subject of novels, here's a novel idea. Always buy hardback novels. You're less likely to buy a book that you've already read and once you're finished reading it, you can do a good deed and get a tax deduction, by donating the book to your favorite charity.

3. Buy a composition notebook, you remember what they look like all decked out in the black and white cover design. Use the notebook to record ideas, note successes, collect inspirational quotes, tape your favorite comic strips, and to write down your frustrations. Keeping this quasi

journal will add dramatically to your professionalism and productivity. People, who write things down, get more done and are less likely to lose track of their good ideas. When was the last time you misplaced a great idea you had because you couldn't remember what it was? Keep your notebook in your briefcase.

4. Create a reading file. Start with a manila file folder and label it reading file. Forget about lugging your favorite magazines around with you. They're getting bigger and heavier with every issue. A recent issue of Fortune Magazine was 542 pages. Now really, who has time to read that? Scan the table of contents and selectively tear out the articles that interest you, staple them, add them to your reading file and toss the rest of the magazine. It's also a superior way to turn waiting time into productive time.

5. Zip it with a Zip Lock bag. Carry a few of these for miscellaneous and convenient tasks. You can use them for holding receipts, holding loose change, batteries etc. You can even use them to hold your Zip and floppy disks.

6. Stay fully charged. Make it a priority to board every plane with fully charged cell phone batteries and notebook batteries. If that's not always practical because of your schedule, consider buying back-up batteries for both.

7. The best is last. Consider getting a PDA. They are simply marvelous and make traveling easier and enable you to be more proactive and more productive on the road. From the palm of your hand you can order a novel from Amazon.com, check ABC news, ESPN Sports, get financial updates from Bloomberg and E-Trade, weather

updates for any city, local traffic for any city, travel directions from MapQuest, restaurant and movie guides for any city, check airline schedules with OAG, check UPS deliveries, and if that's not enough you can send and receive eMails. All of this is wireless and literally in the palm of your hands. Hard to beat and it doesn't weigh a ton. You can also get a fold-a-way keyboard to make typing easier.

Jim Meisenheimer

4 - Time: Make every tick count

Time is of the essence, isn't it? What's important in your professional and personal life? Time is critical and essential to selling success. Unfortunately, time is a limited resource. Don't expect any more than the twenty-four hours each of us is given at the start of every day. This precious time is your daily allotment. You have unlimited choices each day. You can use time or you can waste time. You can prioritize what you will do with your time, or you can let time dribble by and squander it forever.

"Time management" is at best a myth and at worst an oxymoron. You have zero control over the speed of time. You can't speed it up or slow it down. You are relegated to winding up the old grandfather's clock and changing the batteries in your watch. Your control over time is nonexistent. How you use your time is an exercise in self-control. Sadly, most folks don't score well in this category, because it requires discipline and diligence.

Do you know the answers to these questions without having to do the math?

Fifteen minutes is what percent of a twenty-four hour day?

Fifteen minutes is what percent of an eight-hour day?

How many minutes are there in a day?

How many hours are there in a week?

What's the average life expectancy for a male/female?

How much time do you have left?

Most folks don't have a clue to the answers because they macro-manage their time. The macro's waste a lot of time. The micro's compartmentalize everything they do and they typically get more done. The difference between the two is small yet staggering. It's small because minor changes are easy to adopt. It's staggering because these adaptations to your schedule can dramatically change your life forever.

Here's a timely dozen. Twelve ideas, easy to incorporate, that can dramatically impact your selling results, your family and your fun.

1. Set your alarm clock for thirty minutes earlier each day of the week. Do the math and see how much extra time it gives you. How you use the extra time is up to you.

2. Begin every day with a written "To Do" list. Your list should contain all the things you want to do, all the people you want to call, all the phone numbers for all the people you want to call, and the six most important items on your list must be prioritized.

3. Think of your calendar as the center of your life. Identify what's important to you and always put those things on your calendar. Your family belongs on your calendar. Your vacations, exercise, reading, and hobbies

belong there too. If your calendar controls your days, make sure you're headed in the right direction.

4. Build time cushions into your calendar every day. A little elasticity goes a long way in a hectic lifestyle.

5. Read every day. Not reports, but personal growth material. If you don't nurture yourself, you won't grow. Take notes when reading to capture good ideas.

6. Don't let a day go by without asking, "Is there a better way?" If there is a better way, make the changes. Don't wait for someone to hand you a "passport" to enter the world of change.

7. Wear a watch and watch your watch. It's mindless to wear a watch and not pay attention to it. Being on time says a lot about your consistency and credibility. Being late says something too.

8. Delegate more. Forget Lone Ranger selling. Don't do anything if someone else can do it for you. You can't double your sales if you're doing a lot of non-selling stuff. Your highest priority is to be face-to-face with your customers.

9. When you go on vacations don't call the office. They'll survive without you. You'll also send your family a powerful message about their importance.

10. Take good notes. If it's noteworthy, write it down.

11. Buy new technology only when it simplifies your life. You can do without it if it's going to complicate things.

12. Clean your office, your brief case and your car quarterly. Toss out everything that's not essential to your personal and professional life. Clutter is a distraction. It's not about you knowing where something is. Clutter sends the wrong message to everyone who sees it.

Remember, fifteen minutes is 1% of a twenty-four hour day.

Remember, fifteen minutes is 3% of an eight-hour workday.

Remember, there are 1440 minutes in a day.

Remember, there are 168 hours in a week.

Subtract your age from your life expectancy and multiply by twelve to determine your life expectancy in months. Men use seventy-six years and women use seventy-nine years. Don't put off living. Life isn't a dress rehearsal and no one gets out alive. If you pack every day with the right stuff, you'll live a longer and better life.

5 - Self-management

Have you ever thought about things like "getting a grip, getting a life, and having more quiet time?" If you have these thoughts often, you might be out-of-control. Don't worry you're not alone. But what can you do about it? For starters, consider using a watch, an electronic organizer and a daily, weekly, and monthly written plan.

You might be wearing a watch and not using it. A professional is early or on time. If you don't periodically look at your watch to keep you on track and on time, you'll end up being late and rushing. Your watch may be a piece of fine jewelry, but it should function as a timepiece. Divide your day into bite size manageable pieces. Remember fifteen minutes is three percent of an eight-hour day.

Post-it notes are colorful little pieces of paper that are great for reminders and terrible for managing your time and your life. Get an electronic organizer. Any software program that allows you to plan daily, weekly, monthly, and annual events will suffice. Rewriting a daily "To Do" list is unnecessary today. Any task not completed automatically gets added to tomorrow's list. Using a software program to organize your schedule, will automate your record keeping, help with correspondence, and put all customer information at your fingertips.

You must have a written plan. First you need a written plan for your life. Your life, personally and professionally will be chaotic and more stressful without a game plan. Why write down a plan for minor events such as a visit to the grocery store or a list of activities to do on a vacation, and not have a written plan for your life. If you live life one day at a time, I think that's how we do it, it's critical to plan each day carefully. Don't limit your daily plan to a long list of activities; also include quiet time, creative time, exercise time and also family time. You'll feel more in control.

6 - Discombobulated?

Before you throw up your hands and say, "Who, me," remember, it's only natural to occasionally feel anxious, stressed and even frustrated. The key word is occasionally.

There's an old saying that says a problem defined is a problem half solved. There are several telltale signs that may serve as a yellow warning light for you.

Pressed for time - In the complex quick paced world we work in, it's often impossible to get everything accomplished on a daily basis. Our busy schedules can often serve us a double whammy. We schedule too much. We start with the easy things first in order to get them out of the way. Since we can't get everything done we may wind up carrying over high priority and pain-in-the-neck items to the next day adding to the pressure because we failed to get the important things done. Remedy - <u>try to schedule your priorities</u> instead of prioritizing your schedule. Remember first things first and focus on what's important.

At your wits end - Did you ever feel that you had an order locked up, only to learn on the next call that someone with a lot of authority just tossed in a left-handed monkey wrench? You were already planning how to spend your commissions. Now it seems like you're being asked to go back to step one. You might feel like screaming or experience an ordinary sinking feeling. Oftentimes, the situation isn't to blame, we are. Remedy - remember the difference between the trees and the forest. Take a step backwards to move forward. Distance increases your perspective. It doesn't diminish it. Try using pencil and paper to sketch the situation and alternatives for resolving it. There's a real benefit in seeing your problem and options on paper.

Boxed, blocked and caged - There's only one roadblock to closing the deal. From the customer's perspective it's deserved; from your point-of-view it's the last straw and could be a deal-breaker. Examples of what the customer is looking for might include: a request that you beat a competitor's price, a concession in terms and conditions or even a request for a costly product modification. If your experience tells you there's no way out, remember there was a way in. Remedy - creativity and innovation. Make a list of 12 benefits. Make another list that includes five trades you can make with the customer, i.e., if you do this, we'll do this. Just because it feels like your trapped in a cage, don't assume the doors are locked. Shake up your thinking, and you'll stir up the results.

Feeling discombobulated goes with every sales position. Anticipate it and think creatively about how to deal with it when it pays you a visit. It's really an opportunity to deal with adversity and we all know how it feels to triumph over adversity.

7 - Make Time To Find Time

Time is a critical resource. The way most folks squander it, you'd think everyone had more than enough. Why do so many people scream about how much more time they need on the one hand and do so little to manage their time on the other? Managing time is a like brushing your teeth, it's something you have to do every day, and no one can do it for you.

There are all kinds of systems designed to help you manage your time. There are Day Timers, Franklin Planners, and even Time Systems. Each comes with a lesson on how to use it and a portfolio-style book where you are instructed to keep everything except your love letters.

It's not enough to consider time in the traditional day, week, and month framework. To manage your time more wisely, you should view it in smaller increments. Start with fifteen minutes. Most of us think nothing of wasting fifteen minutes. What's fifteen minutes aside from being a small chunk of time? Remember fifteen minutes is 1% of a twenty-four hour day. Squander fifteen minutes and you've wasted 1% of your day. Waste fifteen minutes and you've blown 3% of a typical selling day.

You can't save time like you can money. You can't put fifteen minutes into the cookie jar side-by-side with your loose change. Time can't be saved you can only spend it. How you spend your time is the real challenge.

It's all about how you value, prioritize, use, fill, plan, control, waste, and squander your precious time. There are 168 hours in a week. When asked, most people don't realize how many hours are in a week unless they do the multiplication. Every increment of your time has value. How you use it will contribute to how you are remembered. Here's some time spending ideas.

Invest 1% of each day planning how you will spend the other 99%.

Always ask – what are my priorities?

 Do big things first. Start with the tough stuff.

Do the math to calculate the value (dollars) of fifteen minutes.

If 80% of your sales come from 20% of your customers - allocate your time accordingly.

If 80% of your prospects' potential comes from 20% of your prospects - allocate your time accordingly.

Memorize the difference between being efficient and being effective. It's said to be the difference between doing something right and doing the right thing.

Always focus on being effective.

Before you do anything yourself, consider the value of your time compared to the cost of paying someone else to do it.

The difference between having potential and achieving success is the difference between thinking and doing. Success is all about doing. Nike's theme isn't "do it later." It's "do it now."

You own your time. Don't permit other people to rob you of your time. When you see time robbers approaching say, "gotta run."

Avoid all time traps.

We all live by the same clock, but it's how you wear the watch that makes the real difference. It's not really about making time, though it is about spending it wisely. If you spend most of your time doing what's really important, you will have all the time you ever needed.

Gotta run.

8 - Street Smart Self Management

"To be or not to be" is a great question, isn't it?

An even better question to ask if you want to improve your self-management skills is, "Is it worth doing?" If it is - do it, if it's not - don't.

How come you spend so much time doing so many things that aren't on the top of your priorities list?

How come you're so easily distracted by cell phone calls, eMails, and voice mails?

How come you've never worked harder and longer hours and yet seem to get less done?

When it comes to these issues I'm in the same pickle jar as you. The temptation to get sidetracked is a daily occurrence for me and probably for you.

Here are eight things you can do to maintain your focus so you can achieve your daily, weekly, monthly, and annual goals:

1. Begin every day with a list (must be in writing) of six things to do and six people to call. Use numbers to prioritize your entire list. This is a big one. Think of it as your flight plan for the day.

2. Buy a plastic (see through) file folder. Make sure you print your "To Do" list and make sure it's always the top page in your folder. If you can see your priorities and stay focused throughout the day, the distractions won't stand a chance.

3. Eliminate the drudgery of the routine. For example; do you get eMail requests for quotes, requests for product literature, requests for product returns, requests for service, requests to see you? I'm sure you can add to this list. If you're not already using ShortKeys go to: www.shortkeys.com. You can create and store your eMail responses to common requests and recall the entire message with a keystroke or two. It's a great way handle all repetitive requests and it's only $19.95.

4. Eliminate unnecessary trips to the post office. If you're finding you're spending too much time and making too many trips to the post office invest in a postage meter. It's small and easy to use and usually comes with a built-in weighing scale.

5. How many people have your cell phone telephone number? My guess is probably too many. Everyone who has your cell phone number expects instant access to you. Your cell number becomes the default number, for even routine requests. There's a very high correlation to the number of people who have your cell phone number and the frequency of your daily distractions.

6. Are you practicing safe phone? A word of caution on the proper use of cell phones while your driving. Two of

my clients have said it best. It's against their company policy to use cell phones while driving. The next time you're flying at 30,000 feet, or taking off and landing, how comforting would it be to know that your pilot and co-pilot were on cell phones discussing who knows what.

7. Laminated cue cards can really make a difference. Why reinvent the wheel every day. Salespeople have to secure appointments, ask questions, handle objections, ask for the order, deal with irate customers etc. Put these things down on paper and get it laminated. You'll come across more professional when your sales calls aren't a 100% improvisation.

8. Never, never, never, never lower your price before adding value first. Cutting prices is quick but not profitable for you. Before you utter the words (cost, price, or discount) make certain you have detailed at least three (value and benefit) statements to your potential customer. Adding value reduces the sensitivity to your price. Instead of shooting from the lip with your pricing, bite your lip first and offer (3) benefit statements that relate to your prospect, and save the pricing for last.

To be distracted or not to be distracted is entirely up to you.

"To do or not to do, that's the real question."

If it's worth doing - do it, if it's not - don't.

9 - Handling Paperwork

The one thing about paperwork is that it's endless. All the prognosticators who long ago said that the advent of computers would eventually eliminate paper were totally wrong - at least when I look at my desk. The junk mail you receive is never ending. Add to that correspondence from your company, from your manager, from your customers, personal bills, and everything else under the sun adds up, if you're not very careful, it adds up to one very big distraction.

The control center for most professional salespeople is the home office desk. A desk filled with clutter creates efficiencies that only worsen with more clutter. Here's a suggestion for dealing with paperwork that I personally use and have found to be very effective.

It's called the four D's:

 1. <u>Do something with it</u>. If you can't do something with it right now - you shouldn't be touching the paperwork at all. One of the keys to efficient office management is to touch paperwork only once if at all possible. The best way to do this is to schedule time for the sole purpose of dealing with your paperwork.

2. *Delegate it to someone else*. Delegation isn't easy especially when you know you can perform the task better than someone else. The fact that you can perform the task better than another person is no reason for you to perform the task. First - consider the value of your time. Next - consider the priorities that take precedence over this particular task. Never, never, never do anything that you can get someone else to do for you. Simply stated that's the art of delegation!

3. Defer doing something until you have more time to deal with it. Okay, you have set aside a chunk of time to do your paperwork. One of the items in your stack of paper requires research and follow-up and you estimate that you'll need 45 minutes to get the job done. Defer doing anything until you can block out 45 minutes on your calendar. Just keep moving through your paperwork.

4. Dump it! That's right dump it. My guess is that 20 - 40 percent of everything that crosses your desk can be trashed immediately and without regret. If the worst thing does happen, that you need something you have previously tossed away, worry not, because someone else in your organization will have a copy for you.

All that paperwork that's on your desk doesn't have to be overwhelming. You realize of course that stack of paperwork isn't capable of managing itself. Rely on the four D's to maintain control of your desk. Properly managed your desk will become an asset for you instead of a major liability.

Unfortunately, when it comes to paperwork, you're either in control or out of control. It's your choice.

10 - Reading Books

Do you know how to read books? Really, I'm serious. Most people know how to read yet they haven't discovered the art of reading nonfiction books. Many people look at nonfiction books as an "intimidating activity." In fact, books contain ideas that can be converted into stimulating conversation and often into cash, when you apply the ideas into your business.

Mortimer Adler, a wonderful philosopher, wrote a book called "How To Read A Book" which is an excellent book on how to read books. Yes, it does take time to read a book, but if it's a good book it's always time well spent.

Set a personal goal to purchase one nonfiction book a month. Sure I know you're busy - but don't ever be too busy to get smart. Nonfiction books have a distinct advantage over their rival fiction ones. The advantage is a big one and it's one that will save you lots of time.

Simply stated, the advantage is you do not have to read a nonfiction book cover to cover. As a matter of fact you do not have to begin reading on page one. Nonfiction books usually have a table of contents - so make that your starting point.

When reading, use a Hi-liter to highlight significant passages. You can write the page numbers of these passages on one of the blank pages usually found at the end of the book. When you finish reading the book, review all Hi-lited passages. Take the best thoughts from these books and record them in a composition notebook or dictate your notes into a digital recorder that can be converted to a text file.

Reading does take time - however it doesn't have to take a lot of time. Reading is a busy persons approach to self-education. People become what they read. In time you'll become a more knowledgeable salesperson as your personal library continues to grow.

There are no shortcuts with this subject. No reading - no personal growth. For professional salespeople striving to succeed, reading is never a luxury or an option.

I'd like to spend more time discussing the subject but there is a good book on leadership waiting for me.

11 - Calendars

"To be it or not to be," isn't really **the** question. The question should be paper or electronic. I'm referring to your calendar and the best way to keep tabs on your "To Do" list, your schedule, and all other personal and professional events, that if not organize properly, can take over your life.

The year is 2003. I continue to be amazed, during the sales training seminars I present, how many professional salespeople still control their daily priorities and activities using an old-fashioned calendar that typically weighs three or four pounds. It's stuffed with post it notes and miscellaneous papers that are more distracting than organizing.

From my viewpoint, one of the biggest time wasters is the inability to get organized on a daily basis. If that's true let's get organized. Sure it's going to be painful because it involves change. In this case however change is good.

To get organized electronically you must realize there are numerous options. My time and this space don't allow me the opportunity to review them with you. I'll share two of my favorites. I've been using a Palm Pilot for the last five years. I just started using InfoSelect - (www.miclog.com) in December 2002. I like it so much I'll be loading it onto will allow me to synchronize my desktop computer with my PalmPilot.

Here are some of the advantages of using an electronic "To Do" list and calendar:

1. If you lose your Palm Pilot you buy another one and synchronize it with your desktop computer and you only lose one day's worth of input. If you lose your Franklin planner - you'll lose everything in it.

2. You have immediate access to your calendar, your contact list, and everything else you've entered and stored into your software program. Just think about all the time you spend looking for stuff.

3. You can still print your "To Do" list and calendar. Most people feel that once they switch to a Palm Pilot they are forced to record all notes and observations into the device - which isn't really necessary at all.

4. It changes your perception, rather your customer's perception about you and your organization skills.

When it comes to time most salespeople are on the brink of being out of control and totally stressed-out. It doesn't have to be that way. Time management is an oxymoron because you can't really manage time. You can however manage yourself.

It may be time for a change if you haven't made any changes during the last several years on how you manage your calendar.

12 - Go Take A Long Jump
Off A Short Pier Fund

How many people do you personally know who are having
the time of their lives? Not many probably. How many
people are afraid to take a stand in their work for fear of
losing their jobs?

How many people fail to take a chance because they lack
the financial security required to serve as a springboard to a
new venture? How many people do you know, who
according to Henry David Thoreau, "Live lives of quiet
desperation?" Chances are you know people like this and it
may be a good bet that you're one of them.

Why do so few people ever attempt to unleash the human
potential they possess? You might be surprised at the
answer. For me, it's plain and simple; it's money or more
specifically the lack of it. Money offers options for your
life that empty savings accounts eliminate.

Don't put off "savings" until you feel you can afford to
begin. Paying your rent is an obligation to your landlord.
Setting aside a certain percentage of your income for
savings is obligation to your future. Savings should never
be optional it should be mandatory.

Ideas are a dime a dozen. Acting on them is something else. What's preventing you from sticking to your principles and value system in your current job?

What's preventing you from quitting your job and starting your own business? What's preventing you from moving to a part of the country that you'd like to live instead of living where you're forced to work?

All of these would be easier to consider if you had a "Nest egg " plus a year's worth of living expenses set aside. You'll have more options in your life when you have more money in the back.

If you add up how much time you spend in a lifetime in meetings, traffic, sleeping, and the bathroom, on the phone, doing eMail, you'd be amazed. You would be even more amazed at how much time you're likely to spend in a job that you don't like and one that you're trapped in because you lack the financial resources to make the changes you want to make.

When you have money you can choose how you want to spend your time. When you don't you can't.

Time actually has more value than money. However, the more money you have the more control you have over your time. You can tell anyone to "Go take a long jump off a short pier," only if you have an adequate cash reserve in your "Go take a long jump off a shorter pier savings account."

13 - Mail Call

There's something very special about mail. Think about it for a minute. Six out of every seven days, except for holidays, the United States Post Office delivers your mail personally to your mailbox. In most households and because of schedules one person is generally designated as the official mail retriever.

Because of the long hours most salespeople endure, the mail is usually waiting for you on a table or a kitchen counter top. Even before you kiss your spouse, pat the dog, or greet the kids, you're probably going through your mail. Now I don't want to do an Andy Rooney monologue on the subject of mail, however, I do have a suggestion that may save you some time.

When it comes to mail there are usually piles of it. It becomes the mail game. First we look at it, then we finger through it, then we open up a few pieces and since we don't have much time right now we create another pile or maybe add it to an even larger pile. We stack and re-stack, sort and re-sort, and continue to play the mail game.

The mail is something you get everyday even though you don't have time to deal with it everyday. So here's my time tip and you're probably not going to like it, because it means giving up playing the mail game everyday. As I'm writing this I realize it's Saturday morning. Saturday

Jim Meisenheimer

morning is when I open the mail I've received during the previous week. There's one stack of mail that I can get through very fast because there are no other distractions.

See if it works for you. Open your mail once a week and you'll save a little time everyday.

14 - Why Wait - Create

Someone famous one said, "Don't put off until tomorrow, what you can do today." Procrastination is business/sales enemy #1.

Never before have so many businesspeople and salespeople, been so paralyzed by inaction. It's a form of business constipation. The ability to be decisive is rare, and those who possess it are the last of the breed.

When was the last time waiting got anything done?

When was the last time waiting made you decisive?

When was the last time waiting contributed to the overall G.N.P. in the United States?

When was the last time waiting made you feel good and boosted your ego?

The cumulative impact of waiting is Zippola. Always has been always will be.

Why wait - when you can create? Here's a novel idea. Prepare a written list of all the things you've been putting off or waiting to make a decision on. Include everything from the mundane to the masterful. For example, the mundane - you've put off tidying up your office, especially your desk.

An example of what's masterful could be life changing for you. You've delayed and deferred making a decision about changing jobs or even changing careers.

Once you've created your mundane/masterful list of tomorrows, prioritize every item on your list. There are really only two choices that are now viable for the consummate procrastinator.

1. Do it now!

2. Let it go!

Once you do it now - you'll eliminate the wait and you create. Once you've let it go - you eliminate the excess baggage that you've been carrying around from day-to-day.

Why wait when you can create?

15 - Get A White Board

For the last several years I've toyed with the idea of buying a White Board for my home office. You know the routine, I would think about it then forget about, think about it then forget about it. Four months ago I put it on my To Do list and within 24 hours I ordered my 4'X5' White Board. I also ordered a box of colorful dry erase marking pens.

White Board's are available in various sizes. If you're short on space you can purchase a small one and put it on an easel. When it comes to White Boards size doesn't matter - utility does.

Using a White Board is a no-brainer; I guess that's why it took me so long to buy one. Now that I have one, I can't imagine not having one in my office.

When I'm seated at my desk and look up at my White Board it's perched on the wall like a billboard. Actually, it is a billboard; it's a billboard containing a lot of very important priorities for me and my business.

You can use your White Board in a variety of ways. It's a great way to brainstorm to generate new ideas. Standing up and using multicolored pens seems to get the juices flowing. It can be an excellent motivator on those home office days. What better way to get the most important things done than to be staring at your list of priorities throughout the day?

Using a White Board is a great way to stay focused. It's also the biggest "Reminder" note you will ever come across.

Get a White Board. When you can see your priorities and your goals you will dramatically increase the probability of your success.

16 - Power Cue Cards

Shannon Paxton submitted this time tip.

"Shortly after my daughter turned 16 she received a speeding ticket. We reminded her that one more ticket could result in the loss of her driving license. On her own, she took a bright yellow nail polish and wrote the words 'SLOW DOWN' in large letters across the lower portion of her speedometer, just below the numbers.

Every time she looked to see how fast she was going, she was reminded to slow down. She never mentioned it to us. I saw the message the first time I borrowed her car. You couldn't miss the large yellow letters with baby blue trim - so I even slowed down. By the way, it's been over two years since she got her first and only ticket and her driving record has been perfect ever since."

Isn't that a great story? Well, I believe there's a lesson for teenage drivers and even a subtler message for professional salespeople. What Shannon's daughter did was to create a cue card to adjust her behavior whenever she got behind the steering wheel.

Why not consider some cue cards to modify your behavior on a daily basis when you're in the middle of your sales territory. For example, you could have color-coded cue cards to remind you of the following:

1. Today my goal is to sell $_____.

2. Today I will ask for the order.

3. Today I will not blink or quiver if I hear the dreaded price objection.

4. Today I will follow-up on all customer commitments.

5. Today I will make one more sales call before I call it a day.

6. Today I will maintain a happy face by smiling at everyone I meet.

7. Today will be my best sales day ever.

You get the picture. Having these cue cards handy and visible will serve as excellent reminders throughout your selling day. One of the biggest challenges faced by all professional salespeople is the inability to maintain focus throughout the day.

If Shannon's teenage daughter can change her driving behavior you can certainly change your selling behavior.

17 - Don't Stash It - Trash It

Are you surrounded by stuff? Of course you are - if you're like most salespeople. The tendency, when it comes to stuff, is to wait and procrastinate putting this thing we call "cleaning up" off to a later and more convenient time.

Your mind is probably riddled with these and similar thoughts.

"Not now."

"I'll set aside and take care of it later - when I have more time."

"I'll rack it up by stacking it up in a neat pile."

How would you like to immediately feel good and look good? You're thinking, who wouldn't want to pull a switch to feel good and look good. It's really quite easy and only requires a touch of discipline. Actually, it's as easy as 1, 2, 3. The only thing you need is a large trashcan liner and some "reckless abandon." Here are the easy steps:

1. Trash your office. You will really enjoy doing this - trust me. With your trashcan liner in hand begin with your desk. Without restacking anything toss away everything that isn't absolutely essential to your selling success. Begin at one end of your desk and work your way through to the

other end of your desk tossing away everything that's unnecessary to keep. This includes magazines you haven't read, files that you haven't used, projects that you haven't done, papers that you haven't filed, and notes that you haven't read. The first time you do this can be painful. But remember, if there's no pain there's no gain.

2. Trash your briefcase. Take a couple of pages from your daily newspaper and lay them on the floor. Empty the contents of your briefcase onto the newspaper that's now on the floor. Isn't it amazing, what you have accumulated and stashed away in your briefcase? You know the drill - toss away everything that's not essential to your selling success. Everything else goes back into your now very clean and organized briefcase.

3. Trash your car. The two times your car is the cleanest is the day you buy it and the day you sell it. Depending on what you sell your car may literally become your second office. Your office on wheels can take on the untidiness of your home office if you neglect it.

Start with the trunk - what a mess that can be, and toss away everything that isn't absolutely essential to your selling success. Proceed to your car's interior so you can clean up and toss away everything between and under the seats. Now that you've trashed all the unnecessary stuff - you may as well get the car washed, and even detailed if necessary.

Ask this question often. Should I stash it or trash it? What do you think?

Part II

Managing Your Business

18 - Account Management

There are large accounts and small accounts. The large ones buy more, so I'll emphasize them. The concept is equally well suited for small accounts, but it doesn't pay as much. Think of each of your accounts as a silo. Each silo is filled with opportunities for you. The best way to manage your silos is to begin with a blueprint.

This silo blueprint reveals structure and landscape. Every silo has an organization. A key to successfully working with an account is to discover how it is organized. Start with the company's mission and vision statements. Try to get an organization chart to see the vertical and horizontal layout. Uncover the company's financials to assess underlying strengths and weaknesses. Examine the company's share in the market it serves, and determine their biggest customers and competitors.

Every organization has people. Obtain complete contact information for as many different people that buy, use, influence and make decisions for your product. Get to the decision makers first and get to them early. Decision makers have the power and usually delegate the work.

Sometimes they're more accessible than their staffs, who are busy being worker bees. Always aim high early in the selling cycle.

In your portfolio of account information include key people. Profile the decision makers. Make note of their communication style (dominant, expressive, amiable or analytical) so you can adapt your style to their style.

In large accounts it's easy to focus on a few key people and lose contact with others. Develop a plan for staying connected with everyone in the account. Voice mail and eMail are great tools for staying connected and so are newsletters. If your company doesn't have one yet, don't wait, create your own. Desktop publishing software packages like Quark and Page Maker, with their built-in templates, make this a snap to do and cost effective as well.

When you're working large accounts, always focus on the relationship curve. Where are you in building key relationships? Relationships are built on effective communication, added value, and building trust with people in the silo. Sometimes you can jump-start the relationship building process by getting your key contacts out of their silo. Breakfasts, lunches, dinners, and visits to your company facilities often go a long way in the relationship department and so does a round of golf. Don't make the mistake of spending too much time with too few people. It's strategic suicide to invest too much time with the people who aren't the true decision makers. Start with a blueprint and you'll build better relationships.

19 - Territory Management

There are two critical components to effective territory management and they're as close as kissing cousins. The first is face-to-face time in front of your prospects and customers. The second is routing and scheduling the way you do it. If you're not good at the second, you'll never maximize the first.

Do you know how many days a year you are in front of your prospects and customers? Most salespeople don't keep score and that's a costly mistake. Ignorance is never bliss when it comes to wasting time.

Take a guess. Write down the number of days a year you believe you are in front of your prospects and customers. Use the space provided.

_____

This number represents your perception. What's more important is your reality number. In the space provided enter the number of days.

How many weekend days are there in a year?   _____

How many vacation days do you get each year? ____

How many paid personal and holidays are you entitled to?

_____

How many home office / administrative days do you take a year?   _____

How many days do you spend going to meetings and training programs?   _____

How many sick days do you take each year? _____

How many lost days (weather, canceled appointments, Christmas week) do you take? _____

Total: _____

Add up all these days and subtract from 365. You are left with your reality number. This reality number represents the number of days available to make your numbers. If you multiply your reality number by your average number of daily sales calls, you can calculate your estimated annual sales call numbers.

Once you have calculated total days and total sales calls, you can divide your sales quota dollars by each number. A street smart salesperson knows the value of each day and every sales call, shouldn't you? If you have a variable income, it varies based on performance. Divide your target annual income for this year by the number of days you have available.

You should know how much you earn each day. You can also divide your income goal by the annual number of sales calls you expect to make to derive income per sales call numbers.

If you keep records for your automobile mileage, divide monthly business miles driven by the total number of sales calls made. This will provide you with a - miles per account barometer, which when checked monthly can indicate ups and downs to avoid developing bad habits.

In addition to knowing your numbers there are seven practical steps to managing your territory more effectively.

1. Prioritize all accounts, customers and prospects (Large, Medium and Small).

2. Establish a call frequency schedule for each classification of account - large, medium and small.

3. Determine in advance the percentage of your time you'll commit to prospecting.

4. Change your call pattern to maximize face-to-face selling time.

5. Remember 80% of your revenue comes from 20% of your customers.

6. Remember, 80% of your prospect's potential comes from 20% of your prospects.

7. Never leave home without a map, written call
objectives, and a written territory plan.

Territory management is an essential step to achieving sales
success in your territory. It starts with knowledge. Do the
math to determine where you are currently. Do your very
best to convert driving time to selling time and family time.
Everything around you is changing. It's okay to change
your call schedule, if it makes you more productive. The
customer you always see on Mondays may be a better
customer if you called on him on Thursday afternoons.
You wouldn't let anyone steal your wallet. Don't let
anyone steal your time.

Time is money. It always has been and it always will be.

20 - Reactivity: Quit chasing your tail

Would you rather be proactive or reactive? Next question, which are you, proactive or reactive? Maybe it depends on how you spend your days. Use a quarter to draw a circle in the center of the page on a sheet of paper. Above the circle write the word "button." To the left write the word "reactive" and to the right - write "proactive."

Whoever pushes the button determines whether you're proactive or reactive. If you push the button and begin working on a specific high priority task, you are proactive. If someone else pushes the button and you begin working immediately on his request, without regard and consideration of your priorities, you are reactive.

Under the word "reactive," prepare a list of things that make you reactive. Examples include: your pager starts to vibrate indicating a number for you to call immediately. You check eMails that you don't need to read. A demanding customer makes an unreasonable request. Your manager loads one task upon another on you. If your typical day is like this, don't begin to think you're a proactive person. You're being reactive, if you spend your days responding to the button that other people are pushing.

Under the word "proactive," prepare a list of things to turn these reactive situations into proactive opportunities. When someone calls with a request, politely and firmly let him know what you're working on and when you'll be able to deal with his request. He may not like it, but most folks settle for second best when their first request isn't possible or even practical.

Giving people your pager number is tantamount to telling them they can have instant access to you, which means they can expect to hear from you within an hour. One proud and naive sales rep told me he gave his pager number to 250 customers. Just imagine what his days are like. If you must use a pager, give the number to your spouse, three large customers and three large prospects. When the pager goes off, you'll know it's important.

eMails should be checked twice a day. Like everything else, customer requests should be prioritized. Tell a customer the earliest you'll be able to respond to his request or if possible redirect him to someone else in your company. Don't be the Lone Ranger when dealing with customer requests. Learn to delegate more. Don't ever do something that you can ask someone else in your company to do, simply because you can do it better and quicker.

Reactive people chase around in circles every day instead of focusing their efforts on items of the highest priority. Then they rationalize the energy they've expended by reflecting on how busy they have been.

Nothing produces better results than beginning each day with a six-pack. Your six-pack is a list of six important tasks that you've prioritized for the day. When something happens during the day and hits the fan, don't touch it unless it's more important than your six-pack of priorities.

21 - The Best 15 Minutes Of Every Selling Day

Imagine you are working with your sales manager and as you recap the daily schedule for him, he asks one or more of these questions.

What's the purpose of the sales call?
What do you want to accomplish here today?
Why are we making this call?
What's the reason for the call?
What's the primary sales objective for this call?

How would you respond? Would your response include vague and general comments such as:

To make a sale,
To introduce a product,
To demonstrate a product,
To do a review,
To find out about the customer's needs.

Or would you respond with very specific sales call objectives that are so specific they could pass through an eye of a needle? There are several key advantages to preparing specific sales call objectives for every sales call. But first, when should you plan these objectives? There's no one good time; however, the best planners always try to set aside the same time each day to map out their objectives and strategies.

You may want to devote fifteen minutes at the end of each day preparing the objectives for the next day. Some reps prefer to do it the evening before, and still others like to do it early in the morning.

How specific should you be when planning your sales call objectives? Consider this: how specific would you want to be if you knew there was a high correlation between setting specific objectives and getting results. When you plan exactly what you want to achieve during the sales call, you become incredibly focused and so does the customer.

Here are five reasons why you should spend at least fifteen minutes every day planning specific sales call objectives.

1. You'll achieve "definition of purpose."
2. The objective will direct and guide the call.
3. The customer will know why you're there.
4. Your focused efforts will save wasted time.
5. You'll be able to measure results on every call.

The better your plan, the better your results will be. If you'll invest fifteen minutes every sales day to setting specific call objectives, you will turbo-charge your selling effort and dramatically improve your performance.

Remember... It takes the will to prepare to develop the will to win.

22 - How To Turn Waiting Time Into Productive Time

If you're selling today, it means a good chunk of your time is spent waiting. You wait for customers, managers, callbacks, and planes. Here are seven creative ways to use your waiting time more effectively.

1. Call your extended family. Your call will likely make their day and possibly yours too.

2. Read an article from your reading file. Put all the articles you'd like to read in manila folder labeled Reading File.

3. Using a composition notebook jot down your ideas for pending projects. Use your notebook to periodically record "things that work" during your sales calls. Keep your notebook in your briefcase.

4. Use waiting time to review and prioritize your daily "To Do List" adding and deleting wherever appropriate.

5. Write handwritten thank you notes using a fountain pen. Always carry a supply of note cards and stamps.

6. Expand your network. Use waiting time to call leads, referrals, and anyone else who can expand your business network.

7. Take advantage of your waiting time to listen to your favorite music, read a poem, read Scripture, read a chapter from an unfinished book or take some time just to meditate.

The next time you're waiting for someone or waiting for a delayed flight, consider your options. Waiting time doesn't have to be downtime. Turn your waiting time into productive time.

23 – Pack-rat-itis

You know who you are. You save everything. You feel comforted knowing that if you ever need it, you'll have it. You may be surrounded with piles of paper and information. There really is a better way.

Computers don't save paper, never have and never will. So it's up to you, to effectively deal with the mountains of paper headed your way. Here are several ideas:

1. To most observers, a clear desk is an indication of a clear mind. Likewise, a cluttered desk is never an indication that you are professional and in control of things.

2. Get rid of all paper piles on your desk immediately. Before you hide them, toss away everything that isn't absolutely essential.

3. Keep only three things on your desk (easy to say and hard to do). There are three things to keep on your desk: your planner, your "To Do" list, and the one thing you're currently working on. It's a great way to stay focused.

4. Consider this, if you think you don't need it, you don't need it. Toss it away. This includes out-of-date manuals, catalogs, old magazines, new magazines you'll never read, all third class mail, old files, old equipment, and anything

else you haven't used at least once during the last six months.

5. Once you tidy up your office, you can apply this same magic to your briefcase and your car.

When you fill up a large trashcan liner with unnecessary and unneeded office stuff, you'll know you're headed in the right direction. One of the keys to success is to do this at least quarterly.

"Now, where are those trash can liners?"

24 - How To Achieve Maximum Results In Minimum Time

When it comes to time no one has a net advantage over anyone else, yet most salespeople are extremely frustrated with how little of their time is actually productive. George Stalk, Jr. and Tom Hout, of the Boston Consulting Group, summarize an extensive research program in their book, "Competing Against Time." They discovered that 95 percent or more of the time you classify, as "working on things" is pure waste.

Before I share (10) ideas on how to use your time more wisely, let's review a list of the more common ways salespeople waste time. Here's the list, see if you can add to it:

1. Doing the wrong paperwork - easy stuff first

2. Planning improperly - no written sales call objectives

3. Waiting unproductively - not doing something on your list

4. Failing to qualify the prospect - they're likeable but not profitable

5. Wasting time on small accounts - they could be big some day

6. Handling all problems personally instead of being the quarterback

7. Going to unproductive meetings - because they're fun

8. Checking voice mails too often - because what if it's important

9. Checking eMails too often - ditto above

10. Reading and re-reading your mail - just an old habit

What's the difference between being efficient and being effective: "Being efficient is doing something right. Being effective is doing the right thing."

Consider the impact of doing a job well if unfortunately it was the wrong job or the right job at the wrong time.

Here are six timesaving tips for you:

#1 - Set your alarm clock thirty minutes earlier each day of the week. Do the math and see how much extra time it gives you. How you use the extra time is up to you.

#2 - When it comes to time management here's how you can avoid sounding pathetic. Never say - When would be a good time to see you? How soon do you need it? I know you're busy so I won't take up much of your time.

#3 - Paperwork - Handle paper only once. Don't reach for a piece of paper unless you have time to dispose of it. Do something with it, give it to someone else, toss it out or wait until you have time to handle it.

#4 - Waiting productively - No one likes to wait; yet everyone has to do it. Don't be surprised by it, instead plan for it. You can use this time to write handwritten notes, make customer calls, read a chapter in a book or an article in a magazine and spend time thinking about a big project you're working on.

#5 - Travel tips. Check bags curbside to save time. Tip = $2/bag. You should schedule flights mid-day if possible. Frequent flier status can get you priority check-in and security status. Use one credit card for everything to increase your miles. Consider mailing your luggage to save time. If you have elite status with one airline - you'd be surprised how many other airlines will give it to you. That's how I got my Advantage Platinum and US Airways Gold preferred cards.

#6 - Each day read for fifteen minutes about your selling profession. Create 12 file folders labeled: Time management, negotiating, goals, attitude, territory management, questions, styles, objections, closing, prospecting, telephone, and self-motivation.

Being busy is no substitute for being successful

Two options. One choice.

Time - invest wisely or waste it foolishly. Your call!

Use this space to record your ideas:

25 - Morning Rituals

Throughout my business career my early morning ritual consisted of black coffee and the daily newspaper. I really enjoy the coffee and always looked forward to catching up with the daily news. That all changed in December 2002 when I got a time management tip from Nido Qubein, a very successful businessman and professional speaker. His tip was to forego reading the newspaper in the morning and delay it until the evening. Here's why - you'll achieve more everyday when your day begins more productively.

There are really two reasons for not reading the daily paper in the morning. First, the paper is usually filled with negative stuff, which is not the ideal mindset for professional salespeople. Secondly, depending on how fast you read, it takes valuable time away from the beginning of your day.

Here's a list of five things you can do instead of reading the morning paper:

 1. You can organize your thoughts. That's right, just think about what happened yesterday or what your priorities are for today.

2. You can plan your day by preparing a written "To Do" list. Your days will become more productive when you

begin each one with a written and prioritized list of things you want to achieve.

3. You can prepare and work on specific account strategies for the current day. For every account you're planning to visit you can ask the extremely important "How" question. For example; how will I get the plant tour, how will I uncover the decision makers name, how will I ask for the order etc.

4. You can exercise. You can begin everyday with 20 to 30 minutes of vigorous exercise to reduce stress an increase your personal stamina. It takes a great deal of discipline to exercise on a daily basis. The discipline of daily exercise will reward you with numerous physiological and psychological benefits.

5. You can also invest this time with your family. You decide how to do it.

I still enjoy reading my daily newspaper and I'm finding I enjoy it even more when I do it in the evening. Here's another idea about reading newspapers. Make it a point to identify at least one thing that you can use in your business whenever you read the newspaper. There is always great stuff in the sports and business sections.

The world is filled with ideas you can use to grow your business - just keep your eyes open to avoid missing them.

26 - Business Travel Tips

The harsh reality today is that business travel isn't fun. While that may be true it shouldn't mean it can't be productive for you. Here are a few tips to make your next business trip a little more productive.

Pick the best flights. Picking the best flights means different things to different people. For me the best flight is a flight that gets me to my destination between 5 and 6 PM. First of all, if there's any kind of a delay or problem with the plane - I have a better opportunity to schedule another flight during the same day. Flying at this time also allows me to get settled into my hotel and enjoy dinner at my normal dinnertime. Since I fly a lot, but not as much as the1K flyers do, there's less competition for first-class upgrades during these mid afternoon flights.

Pack the right stuff. Once again packing the right stuff is like picking the best flights and will vary from person-to-person. For me, the right stuff is less stuff. Unless I'm traveling for more than two days I'll pack a suitcase I carry on the plane. I always back a good book and lately I've been packing two good books - because of the increase waiting time at the airport and sometimes on the plane. I always travel with Rockport walking shoes - which are the most comfortable shoes on the planet. I also pack some exercise equipment. Not much and nothing fancy. I include two hand grippers and latex tubing with handles at each end. It's a great reminder for me that exercise should be done on the road.

Portable office. My portable office includes a notebook computer, PalmPilot, cell phone, legal pad, and see-through file folders. These folders allow easy access to my important stuff. You can order them from Century Business Solutions 800-767-0777. When ordering specify Century-Safe Paperwork Arrangers.

Work and play. My attitude about flying is that it shouldn't be all work. Usually, I try to split by work time and play time 50-50 whenever I fly. Some people enjoy movies, some people enjoy CDs, and I enjoy reading mysteries. So, the last half of every flight is devoted to devouring another whodunit.

Expense control. I try to keep tabs on what I spend while I'm spending it. I have created a template that I print on a standard size envelope. It includes the date, customers named, and spaces for the following: airfare, hotel, meals, taxi, miscellaneous, shipping etc. as I incur the expense I write the amounts on the outside of the envelope and put the receipt on the inside. It's simple and easy.

When traveling I don't want to be the road warrior - I prefer to enjoy the ride as much as I can. These tips work for me and I hope they work for you.

27 - Using Technology
To Achieve Balance

This chapter is about balance. It's about maintaining equilibrium between your professional and personal life. From my perspective the critical measurement is time and I'd like to share with you some ideas on how using technology in your professional life can increase the time you have for your personal life. Here we go:

1. Technology should simplify not complicate your work.

2. Today, typing 35 words minute just doesn't cut it. So I rely on Dragon System's voice activation software - which enables me to type 150 words a minute hands-free. **More about this in the next chapter**.

3. I save 125 hours a year, more than three weeks, by not running to the post office on a daily basis. My postage meter is fast and reliable.

4. When you make your electronic calendar the centerpiece of your life you'll do what's important first. Get rid of those old-fashioned daily planners and calendars.

5. I just purchased InfoSelect software, which can be purchased and downloaded from http://www.miclog.com. It is a personal information manager that organizes internet

data, notes, To Do's, schedules, contacts, addresses, forms, ideas and more. This software is incredible.

6. If your business is like my business there are lots of routine tasks to deal with. Instead of typing or even cutting and pasting I can set up paragraphs with only a few keystrokes by using the software from http://www.shortkeys.com. It's a big timesaver.

7. You don't need high-tech to save time. I purchased a 3'x 4'whiteboard for my office. My whiteboard allows me to imaginize, strategize, and visualize what's important on a daily basis. Seeing my priorities on this whiteboard is like having them up on a marquee in neon lights.

8. Start every business day with a list of the 6 most important priorities for that day. Always in writing.

9. Don't give your cell phone number to anyone. This includes eliminating "and if it's an emergency - here's my cell phone number" from your voicemail message. The quickest way to lose sight of your priorities is to give scores of people instant access to you. Being tethered to your cell phone doesn't make you proactive - it makes you reactive.

10. Minimize playing telephone tag by asking for a caller's eMail address in your voicemail message. 75 percent of the callers leave their eMail addresses making it easier for me to connect with them.

11. You can put your whole life on a PalmPilot. Enough said!

12. It's important to backup all computer files. There are many ways to do this and most of them are time-consuming. I rely on http://www.connected.com. Once a night they come in and visit my system and copy all new and all changed files. You won't believe the price.

13. If you need help for special projects consider using http://www.elance.com. You can post - literally any job requirement you have, set any parameters you want, and expect to have a lot of people bidding on your project. I have used them twice with very good results.

14. Here's another big time saver. Publish a weekly (eMail) newsletter. Once a week my newsletter is eMailed to 27,000 subscribers. Some of them are customers and prospects. I'm not sure if there is an easier and more cost effective way to communicate with that many people on a weekly basis.

As golfer Bobby Nichols once said, "When you think you've got it in this game, that's when you've had it." I keep trying new things and encourage you to do the same.

The more you rely on technology, the more time you'll have for balance in your life.

Balance just doesn't happen – you have to make it happen.

28 - Hands-free Typing

When I was in high school I got some very bad advice. My guidance counselor advised me to skip the typing class and encouraged me to take physics instead. Well, I've never really had to apply anything I learned in that physics class but there is not a day that goes by that I wish I could type faster.

Let's face it, typing 35 words a minute in this fast pace world, is a handicap. Sure I've tried to fix the problem several times. I purchased the Mavis Bacon Typing software program and used it to no avail. Taking 30 minutes a day to practice something I should have learned in high school just doesn't make sense.

I usually spend two weeks following the lessons and then run into a wall filied with deadlines. What happens then is no surprise. I scrap the lessons and tackle my list of A priorities.

You're probably thinking I'm destined to spend the rest of my life typing 35 words a minute with my two fastest fingers. Not so, say the promoters of Dragon Systems software. They say you can literally type as many as 150 words a minute hands-free.

Now, do I like the sound of that? I won't get in to all the details of how the program works - but rest assured the program works. And the more you use it the better it gets. Here's a short list of things you can do with voice activation software on a daily basis:

1. "To Do Lists."

2. Add contact information to your database.

3. Send eMail's via Outlook.

4. You can write those million dollar proposals.

5. Write letters.

6. Enter data in an Excel spreadsheet.

7. Record your notes from a sales call.

8. Makes up pre-call planning easier to do.

9. Plus a whole lot more...

You can type 35 words a minute like a two fingered wounded alien or you can invest in the Dragon Systems software program and type as fast as you can talk. Do you have any idea how fast that is if you're from New York?

This software program is easy to use and easy to get used to. If you try it you won't be disappointed.

Jim Meisenheimer

29 - Double The Probability

Have you ever missed a telephone call? You know, you're out making sales calls, running errands or even on another telephone call. When that call comes in and goes to voice mail it sets in motion the game of "telephone tag." And what a game it is.

Telephone tag at its best is time-consuming and at its worst a real pain in the butt. It's virtually impossible to eliminate telephone tag but there is something you can do to keep it at a minimum. Here's my idea and it has to do with your voice mail message.

First, let's start at the beginning when it comes to recording your voicemail message. There are three things to keep in mind:

1. Avoid changing your message everyday. You run the risk of not recording your best message and you run the risk of forgetting to change it.

2. Place a mirror, approximately 5 by 7 inches, behind the phone. Make sure your smiling whenever you reach for the telephone.

3. When recording your message say it slowly and energetically. You might want to even consider standing

up while you're recording this very important voicemail message.

Most messages end up pretty similar, sounding like this:

"Hello, this is Jim Meisenheimer.

I'm either on the other line or out of the office.

Please leave your name, telephone number, and a detailed message.

I'll call you back as soon as possible."

That's a pretty standard voicemail message that most people encounter on a daily basis. What you get is what you ask for namely the telephone number and a brief message.

Let's make one change and see what happens:

"Hello, this is Jim Meisenheimer. I'm either on the other line or out of the office. Please leave your name, telephone number, a detailed message and your eMail address to make sure we can connect as soon as possible. Thank you for calling."

It's my experience that about 75 percent of all callers leave their eMail addresses. Now you have a telephone number and an eMail address thus doubling the probability of connecting with your caller.

There's another benefit to using this approach. Your message is different than all the others. Anytime you can do something that stands out it's a built-in benefit for you. Make sure your voicemail message is the very best you can make it.

30 - Goodnight Chet . . .

During the 1950s and '60s Chet Huntley and David Brinkley, the famed Evening News duo, graced the NBC network for years with their evening nightly program. One of the things that made the program so different was they didn't share the same television studio. In fact one of them broadcast his report from New York City and the other from Washington D.C.

Regardless of the news report, you could always count on their signature sign off at the end of the show. It would go like this, "Goodnight Chet," and "Goodnight David" and "Goodnight for NBC News." It was practical and it worked.

A signature sign off can also work in your sales effort. You too can benefit from a signature sign off in all your eMail correspondence. Here are three reasons why you might benefit from a prepared eMail signature:

1. You'll save time if you prepare your eMail signature in advance.

Not only will you save time, your eMail will look more professional whenever you prepare your eMail signature in advance. There is something naked about an eMail with just a name in the signature line.

2. Your eMail signature can also establish a personal brand for you.

Your eMail signature gives you an opportunity to do some personal branding. For example, if you've been an equipment specialist for 23 years why not include that in your eMail signature. It's very subtle, yet it reminds everyone with every eMail, that you are and equipment specialists and you have been one for 23 years. It's practical and powerful.

3. If your eMail signature contains the right stuff it may also save your customers and prospects time.

You should include the following in your eMail signature: your name, telephone number, web site, personal branding statement, and a P.S. designed to promote one of your products or services.

Here's an example of my current eMail signature.

Jim Meisenheimer
Sales Strategist

(800) -266-1268
website: www.meisenheimer.com

P.S. Don't forget to register for my next TeleSeminar.

Color is added for emphasis (Sales Strategist is in dark blue.) You don't have to be a famed NBC commentator to have your own signature sign off. Goodnight Chet and goodnight David and thanks for a great idea.

31 - The Art of Of Saying No

What could be easier than saying no? Apparently everything, because so few people are able to say it with any regularity. Here are several reasons:

There's something irreverent about saying no.

There's something impolite about saying no.

There's something disrespectful about saying no.

There's something naughty about saying no.

Think about it this way. When you refuse to say no you're actually saying yes. Consider what happens to your life when you refuse to say no to:

  -- Routine customer requests

  -- Ordinary management requests

  -- Last-minute family requests

  -- Spontaneous requests from friends

Better you should wear a facial tattoo that says, "I'm available for any request (reasonable or unreasonable) on a

24/7 basis. Forget about the tattoo think about responding with these alternative phrases.

1. I'm not able to do that, but I know just the person who can help you with that right now.

2. I'm not able to do that for you, here's what I can do though.

3. Based on my schedule, the earliest I can do that for you is Thursday morning. How would that work?

4. No. (Sometimes you have to be direct.)

Saying no needn't paralyze you. Let's face it you can't do everything everybody wants all the time. If that's true it means you'll have to develop the courage to say no once in a while.

The easiest way to become a nay-sayer is to prepare and practice what you'll say and how you'll say it. You'll soon develop an energizing confidence, by itself; will eliminate numerous requests before they ever get asked.

The art of saying no begins with knowing how to do it. Just say no if you want to become unburdened and liberated from untimely requests for your precious time.

32 - Delete Key

The most powerful key on your computer keyboard is the Delete key. It's not the Enter key, it's not the Control key, it's not the Shift key, it's not the Alt key, and it's certainly not the Backspace key. The most powerful key is truly your Delete key.

When you add Spam to your corporate eMails you're probably faced with an overwhelming barrage of daily eMails. Use the Delete key whenever you don't need to open the eMail. If there is any doubt in your mind press the Delete key. If you open an eMail and discover you don't need to finish reading it simply Delete it.

When it comes to eMails you have several options and they include:

1. You can *Delete* it immediately. You can probably do this twice as much as you are doing it now.

2. You can wisely forward it to someone else.

3. You can file it.

4. You can save it for later.

When in doubt most people are likely to save their eMails. I suggest when in doubt Delete the eMails.

You'll increase your productivity substantially when you use the Delete key for all nonessential eMails.

When you have the power to Delete why in the world would you choose any other options?

33 - Delegate To Relegate

First, let's go to the dictionary and see what these words really mean.

The word delegate means, according to The Random House College Dictionary, to designate a person to act for or represent you, to send or appoint a person as deputy or representative, to commit (Powers, functions, etc.) to another person.

The word, relegate, means to send or consign to an inferior position, place, or condition. It also means to send into exile and to banish.

Now that we have the definitions clearly established let's give them a selling perspective. In sales, a salesperson's most precious commodity is time. Whenever you do something, regardless of the reason, that somebody else in your company can do, you're wasting your valuable time.

Always remember - never do anything that you can get someone else to do for you. The reasons are quite clear and very simple:

1. Selling time is prime time. Your priority is to sell not to fix.

2. When you delegate you empower others and that creates trust.

3. When you do it yourself you'll have less time for selling and little time to create trust among your fellow employees.

When it comes to delegation, throw rational reasoning out the window. Your time matters most. And your time in front of customers matters even more.

It doesn't matter that the task is very important.

It doesn't matter that you can do the task better than another person.

It doesn't matter that you can do the task quicker than another person.

It doesn't matter that the task won't take long to complete.

What does matter is your time.

What does matter is how you spend it.

What does matter is how you prioritize the things you do and the things you decide not to do.

What does matter is that you'll achieve better selling results by doing less and selling more.

Acting as a Lone Ranger in your territory will definitely have a negative impact on your selling results. The more you delegate the more likable you'll become. The more you delegate the more you will achieve. Both are excellent reasons for you not doing it.

When you don't delegate properly you end up doing things someone else should be doing.

When you delegate you relegate those tasks to someone else.

Finally, the more you delegate, the more (important stuff) you'll actually get done.

So what are you waiting for - give that task to someone else and do it right now.

34 - The Key To Finishing Is Starting

Recently I did a postcard mailing to promote my Advanced Selling Skills Boot Camp. One side of the postcard had a photograph of a salesperson, dressed in a suit, running, with both arms extended high over his head, one with a briefcase, as he dashed across a red ribbon finish line.

It was a great picture capturing a successful moment. It reminded me, and I don't know why, that you'll never cross the finish line until you cross the starting line.

How many things are you thinking about doing that aren't getting done?

How many priorities do you have perched on the back burner in your territory?

How many things could you start doing today that would provide you with an immediate payback ($$$)?

If finished is better than perfect then starting is better than procrastination.

Before you cross the finish line you have to cross the starting line.

(Begin, dart, spring, jump, effect, enable, rouse, proceed, an outburst.) What are you waiting for?

35 - Schmoozing Is Losing

Isn't that a great title? If you schmooze too much you end up losing a lot. When you're schmoozing you're engaged in unproductive and unrewarding conversation. Literally, it means to chat idly and to gossip. Schmoozing takes time and wastes time. Considering how this book is all about using time more productively you can imagine that schmoozing is not one of my favorite pastimes.

Schmoozing can be segmented. For example in sales there are four basic types of schmoozing:

1. <u>Phone schmoozing</u>. Some people define themselves by the number of minutes they see on the telephone bill at the end of the month. They just can't do enough telephone talk. It's hard to schmooze on the telephone and be in front of customers at the same time. The fact that phone schmoozing is enjoyable doesn't make it desirable.

2. <u>Customer schmoozing</u>. Some schmoozing is appropriate but too many salespeople cross the line too many times. Unless your customer is into schmoozing, it can have a negative impact on your relationship. Consider what's appropriate and stick to it.

3. <u>Buddy schmoozing</u>. Now this should clearly be off-limits during the business day. If you're popular you probably have a wide circle of friends - and that's good for

you. There is however no need to work your circle of friends during the business day, which only leads to missed sales opportunities.

4. <u>Incessant schmoozing</u>. These are people who love to talk - and when they're alone they talk to themselves. This is incessant schmoozing. What schmoozers don't understand is when people see them coming they run for cover. If you're an incessant schmoozer get a job at the telephone company.

If you're a schmoozer it's probably an indication of poor planning. The more organized you are the less schmoozing you're apt to do. Sometimes your schmoozing is a direct result of your behavioral style. Hippocrates was the first to point out four dominant styles. One of these styles is the expressive. Expressive people love the chit chatting, talking, discussing, and even arguing.

Not all schmoozing is bad. Likewise not all schmoozing is good. Too much schmoozing inhibits your selling results. Too little schmoozing may inhibit your customer relationships. So it's important to consider a balance when comes to schmoozing.

Increasing your schmoozing time won't increase your selling results and may have a negative impact on them. The remedy for schmoozing is an old-fashioned timer. You don't have to give up schmoozing entirely, just keep a lid on it by setting a timer to it.

Just remember schmoozing eats up valuable selling time. It may feel good but it doesn't help you to be good.

36 - Prioritizing Makes You Enterprising

Everybody is so busy doing things that don't really matter wouldn't you agree? We answer, the always-ringing telephone, respond to a growing list of eMails, and give immediate knee-jerk responses to all customer and management requests.

Yada, yada, yada, and the beat goes on. But, the beat doesn't have to go on. You don't have to live your life in the reactive mode. There is an option and it's called being proactive. Proactive salespeople are always working on their highest priorities by choice not chance.

Today, priorities do matter. Do what's important first. If you always do what's important first you'll always work more effectively and achieve better selling results. You'll become a giant among your selling peers based on your improving results and overall accomplishments.

The key to prioritizing is making lists and then prioritizing them using numbers. These lists should include:

⇒ Daily "To Do" lists

⇒ Annual goals list

⇒ Prospect lists

⇒ Customer lists

⇒ Proposal list

⇒ New projects list

Creating lists that are prioritized sounds mundane but it's not. These lists will keep you focused on what's really important. When you're working on what's important the daily interruptions and distractions get neutralized - and don't stand a chance of getting in your way.

Prioritizing is the quickest pathway to getting things done. Prioritizing really does make you enterprising.

Part III

Managing How You Sell

37 - Breakfast For Champions

I heard Tom Winninger, former president of the National Speakers' Association, once declare that you can't succeed alone. If you're a solo practitioner like me or outside salesperson like you, it's easy to believe that we matter most. Three years ago I was reminded again how important it is to have good and productive working relationships with people outside of your principle business. Here's what happened.

A former customer and now good friend Bill Y. and I periodically get together for early-morning breakfasts. Bill has a great track record working with two Fortune 500 companies. Today he's an entrepreneur growing his own company.

During a phone call we discussed the place and a time for our upcoming breakfast. The last thing Bill said to me was, "I'll be on time." Those of you who know me know that I'm organized and punctual. Nevertheless, his final words stayed with me until our meeting on Friday.

I got to our meeting, which was five minutes from my home, seven minutes early. He got to our meeting 45 minutes early. He used the time to catch up on some early-morning business reading.

His commitment to "be on time" increased my own awareness and heightened my commitment not to let him down.

According to my national survey "not having enough time" is one of the biggest challenges you face everyday. Waiting time is a big piece of your downtime. If you'd like to minimize your downtime try using "I'll be on time" whenever you schedule appointments. It really works.

When Bill and I get together for breakfast it's not really about networking and brainstorming. It's about "brain-stilling." On a typical day my brain is already storming. Periodically, I believe it's okay to slow things down a little. It's opportunity to share ideas, give and get feedback, and of course have a few laughs.

Soon after we got together, I said to Bill "I need your advice." I wanted his feedback on a new program I was developing. I got more than I bargained for.

At one point during breakfast he got up went to the cashier and came back with envelope. When breakfast was over there was six ideas scribbled on the back and front of that envelope.

If I implement these ideas I believe they will add $50,000 of increased revenue within 12 months to my business.

When the pace is quick, the schedule is full, time is short, and your to-do list is a mile long, having breakfast with a friend may not be a high priority for you. Likewise when the pace is quick, the schedule is full, time is short, and your to-do list is a mile long, it's easy to work with your head stuck in the sand.

I can't begin to tell you how energizing that breakfast was for me. It could be that way for you too, so pick up the telephone and invite a friend to an early-morning breakfast.

Remember that distance creates perspective. People who are not in your business often see things differently and certainly more clearly than you. When it came, I lunged for the check. I'll be buying Bill breakfasts for a very long time.

Here's a great way to jump-start the final trimester of the calendar year. Create a list of all the things you do as a professional salesperson. For example sales call planning, goal setting, asking questions, handling objections, eMail, voicemail, closing, networking, time management etc.

Once your list is complete ask yourself the following question "is there a better way to do it?" If there is, make the appropriate changes.

Also, if you can change one thing about the way you sell, what would have the biggest positive impact on your results?

Champions acknowledge what's holding them back (weaknesses) and develop a plan for improving them in a systematic way.

Use this space to record your ideas:

38 - Eliminate Watch Watchers

During a presentation, usually when you're speaking, have you ever caught a potential customer trying to sneak a peak at his watch? Of course, you have, and so have I, up until I made a discovery. What I learned was that potential customers looked at their watches when I was talking, not when they were talking. They always become more interested in any subject when they are the ones doing the talking.

And the more they talk, the less likely they'll be to look at their watches. And as a matter of fact, I've never seen potential or actual customers look at their watches when they were talking.

Another reason to get your customers talking is that if they're spending less time looking at their watches, you'll get more quality time with them.

If you want more quality time with your prospects and customers always ask really good open-ended questions. The better the question, the more you'll learn about the person you're talking to.

Watches tell time. They don't determine how much of it a customer will give you. Getting more time depends less on what you say and more about the questions you ask.

39 - Sales Call Management

What is your response to this question, "What's your recipe for selling?" Do you have a response? Do you abide by a formal sales process? Does it consist of multiple steps that are thoughtfully mapped out in writing? Does this sales process suit you and fit your products? What percentage of your sales calls are prepared versus improvised?

I'd like to share my sales process with you. It's easy to use and hard to do without. It has seven steps, each one different from the other yet very much connected.

1. The selling process always begins with networking. To build your network, you must cast the net. All fishermen understand that fish don't jump onto boats voluntarily.

2. The selling process always asks the right questions. A sales person without questions is like a comedian without jokes. Questions if used properly get you off the hook. No salesperson worth his salt wants to talk about products before he knows what the customer needs. Asking questions, open-ended ones, gets the job done.

3. The selling process always depends on effective listening. Listening is activated in two ways. First, it kicks in whenever you ask a really good question. Second, once you've asked your question your listening is also activated by closing your mouth. When the mouth is in the closed

position, the ears work wonderfully. Another way to boost your listening skills is to take notes.

4. The selling process always uncovers specific problems and opportunities. Unlike most doctors, salespeople seem to prefer talking about their prescriptions before they do the examination. Be like a doctor. Do the exam, before you offer your product as the cure.

5. The selling process always presents tailored solutions. One size never fits all so present only tailor-made solutions to your customers. This involves doing more homework initially. Don't leave a customer trying to imagine if your product will work. Show him specifically, in the context of his problems, how your product works to his advantage. A sale occurs when your product solves the customer's specific problem. It's the "relatability" factor. Before the customer can relate to your product, you must relate to his problem or special situation.

6. The selling process always deals with concerns. There are four universal objections. No money, no need, no hurry, and no confidence. Conceptually, learn how to deal with each. The best objections to get are the ones you get often. Recurring objections are gifts, because you know you'll get them over and over. You can't prepare for the objection you haven't heard before. You can prepare and practice for the one you'll hear again tomorrow. How could you intelligently not want to prepare for an objection you know you'll hear again, probably next week?

7. The selling process always secures the commitment. Asking for the business doesn't take guts, it takes know-

how. When it's time to ask for the business, how specifically do you ask? If you have to think about it, it means you don't know. There are no techniques for asking for the business, only words. Think about the words you'll use. Write them down on a sheet of paper. Play with the words. Only keep the words that are essential. Recite them out loud. Listen to how they sound.

You'll know when you have the best combination of words. It'll sound like music. Before you get to the account, rehearse these words a minimum of six times. Keep doing it until you can do it without inserting any "um's" and "ah's". Imagine how good you'll feel and sound, when you're in front of the customer. You'll be extremely confident, because you've already practiced it six times. Going for the order shouldn't create anxiety; it should get you the business.

The selling process is just that - a process. It's not a mish mash, an improvisation or a comedy act. It always starts with your customer and ideally ends with your product positioned as a tailor-made solution. The secret to success is to balance preparation with spontaneity, to do the homework before taking the exam and to realize that selling is more about skills than instinct.

40 - Learning Behind The Wheel

When it comes to cars and driving, one thing is certain; the roads aren't getting wider and faster. The cars themselves are getting better, more comfortable, more luxurious and filled with the latest gadgets. Aren't we fortunate, considering how much time we spend behind the wheel?

We do everything in cars don't we? The professional sales representative certainly does. Consider the inconspicuous trunk. For a sales rep it becomes a sealed office holding files, samples, company literature, computer disks as well as the spare tire.

Many people are eating one or more meals in their cars. Some of us like to relax and listen to our favorite music or radio talk show. We can make telephone calls, send FAXES and yes even use our notebook computers.

How many of us though, are learning in our cars? What would be the personal and professional impact if we invested only 1% of our lives listening to motivational, inspirational and educational tapes while driving our cars? Look at it this way. How much of our adult lives should be dedicated to learning?

Since we're spending more time in our cars, shouldn't we spend some of it more productively? The audiocassette tape has revolutionized the opportunities for self-development.

self-development. With books on tape, speeches on tape and focused training programs on tape. Now more than ever, it's possible to turn driving dead time into productive learning time.

Experts tell us to get the real benefit from an audio tape it should be replayed to allow key points to be reinforced. This repetition is essential to the learning process.

When you invest 15 minutes a day to your personal development it represents 1% of your life. Another way to view this is to consider what kind of person you can become if you committed 15 minutes each day listening to audiocassette tapes related to the field of professional selling.

To activate your tape library check out my website – www.meisenheimer.com.

Take advantage of those increasing driving times. Turn your radios off, turn your tapes on, and if you do this consistently, you'll develop a very significant strategic selling advantage over your competition.

41 - Asking For The Order

Learning occurs when students learn from their teachers.
Sometimes teachers learn as much from their students.
Here's an example.

Four years ago I conducted a two-day sales training
program for one of my clients. There were 23 salespeople
in the class. One of the exercises we did classified
behavioral styles for the participants. "D" is for driver or
dominant, "I" is for influencer or expressive and so on.
Another exercise focused on the importance of asking for
the order.

Here is an eMail I received five days after the program
from, Michael, one of the participants.

Steve and I (He was the "D" and I was the "I") arrived
early at the airport, for our flight back to Newark. As the
skycap delivered our bags to the then-empty counter, I
picked up on the fact that the ticket agent, named Candace,
was not having a good day. After a bit of "I" style banter,
we discovered that just prior to our arrival, Candace had to
deal with an irate customer, who was yelling and screaming
at her because he wasn't allowed to carry four bags on his
flight.

The incident was so bad she had to call security. She
wasn't prepared for another confrontation. She was,

however, genuinely surprised and pleased that both of us were concerned about her, as we offered her words of encouragement (but not platitudes).

That's when Steve the "D" guy got involved. Candace had mentioned that our flight wasn't very full, so Steve asked, "Can we be upgraded to First Class for free?"

After what seemed to be an eternity of dead silence, Candace took our coach tickets, ran them back through the computer, and stamped "First Class" on them. It was as simple as that.

We ran into a few of our classmates at the Pittsburgh airport, grumbling about Friday flight delays and cancellations they were experiencing. Our flight was delayed one hour, but we didn't care at that point, we were flying First Class. We didn't get the hot towels we anticipated, but we did learn an important lesson. The lesson is "Always ask for the order." It's a lesson we won't forget.

It's one thing to take a class and it's quite another to immediately begin applying what you just learned.

In the classroom, everyone has the opportunity to be a teacher and a student. If you don't know that you don't know and are unwilling to experiment with new ideas you may never reach the "First Class" level of professional selling.

42 - The Most Powerful Word In Sales

Would you like to raise the bar on your sales performance and results? Would you like to earn more money? Would you like to enjoy greater success in your career? It's all yours for the ASKING. It's literally all yours for the ASKING.

Would you like to get more done in less time?

The most powerful word in sales is the word - ASK. If you ask more, you'll achieve more. Sounds simple, but it's not easy. Here's a short list of what to ASK for.

ASK for the first appointment.

ASK really good questions to uncover needs during that first meeting.

ASK for a tour of their facilities to show your interest and to increase your opportunity to meet other people.

ASK to present your solutions/benefits package to the entire committee.

ASK to arrange a hands-on demonstration of your product.

ASK for the follow-up appointment before you leave.

ASK for the order and offer options to choose from.

ASK for the order again, if you first have to handle objections.

ASK for their commitment to an extended service contract.

ASK for a minimum of three referrals.

ASK every satisfied customer for testimonial letters or eMails.

ASK your customers to evaluate your performance quarterly.

ASK them for more business.

ASK them for even more business.

When salespeople hesitate to ask, they do so because they have anxiety, lack confidence, and haven't prepared (word for word) what they will say in these situations. The time to prepare is definitely not when you're in front of the customer.

When you combine preparation with practice (out loud) you're on your way to achieving better results. The anxiety is gone, confidence is boosted, and your customer is more likely to respond more favorably to your professional approach. **ASK**ing more will help you achieve more. Preparing what you ask and practicing how you ask will give you superior results.

43 - The Quickest Way To Increase Sales

The quickest way to increase sales is to make things happen - not to let things happen. Let me explain.

You can speed up the selling process and decrease the selling cycle time when you have a written game plan. Your game plan should include three key elements. These elements are your objectives, the strategies, and your tactics.

Your objectives and for these priority accounts should include what you want to sell, how much you want to sell, and when you want to sell it by. The "what you want to sell" includes the mix of products that make the most sense for your prospects situation. The "how much you want to sell" is the dollar value of this product mix. The "when you want to sell it by" is your target date for asking for the prospects commitment to purchasing their products.

The strategies explain "How" you're planning to achieve your objectives. The key to developing strategies is to have enough of them. Remember, strategies answer the question "How."

How #1

How #2

How #3

How #4

How #5

As you develop your strategies keep asking this very important question. **What's the probability of success if I only do How #1?** What's the probability of success if I only do the How #1 and How #2? What's the probability of success if I only do How #1, How #2, and How #3? You get the picture. When the answer to your probability question equals 85 percent you're ready for action.

Tactics are the details. We all know how important details are, and if you're not careful they can sabotage even the best plans. Each strategy has subordinate details. For example, if you have an entertainment strategy here are some of the details you would want to consider.

- Who - who will go to the dinner?

- Which - which restaurant will be selected?

- When - when will we go to the restaurant?

- How - how will we get there?

- What - what are the priorities to be discussed at dinner?

Think about how your selling process can be accelerated when you have a simple yet powerful game plan. Your game plan should be in writing. Your game plan doesn't have to be complicated and won't be time-consuming if you put it all on one-page.

Your one-page strategic account plan is your ticket to a faster sale. Naturally, a quicker sale takes less time.

Use this space to record your ideas:

44 - Say It With Class

How you say thank you to your customers says an awful lot about you. In this mad-dash world we live in, where the pace is fast and insensitivity to others is at all-time high I have a radical idea for you to consider.

Why not say thank you with a hand written note? I know what you're thinking - that's going to take too much time and I already don't have any time to spare. Nothing is further from the truth. If you knew something you did would put a smile on a customer/prospect's face almost every time - would you do it? Of course you would.

You can write a two sentence, 21 word hand written note, and address the envelope in 47 seconds. Don't challenge me on that because I just timed it. Look, we live in a high-tech global world economy. Any effort you make to do "High Touch" things will stand out like positive banner advertising. The thing about writing handwritten notes is you can always make them short and sweet. Here's an example:

Date

Bill:

Thanks a million for the plant tour. I'm sending you the literature you ask for. See you February 5th.

Your signature

It's that simple. Imagine getting into the habit of writing to 5 notes a day. That's 25 a week. That's 1250 a year. Imagine writing your notes with a fountain pen. Imagine using brightly colored envelopes - so they stand out. Imagine putting a smile on your customer's face - because you do that whenever you say thank you.

Here is a resource for you. The name of the Company is IntroKnocks. Their specialty is professional business greeting cards. They have an absolutely and positively unbelievable selection of cards. You can call them for a catalog at 800-753-0590. You could also visit their web site (www.introknocks.com)

From your customers perspective here's how you benefit:

{ Your handwritten note creates a "High Touch" impact.

{ Your handwritten note is a personalized and thoughtful message.

{ Your handwritten note screams First Class.

{ Your hand written note takes less time to write that it does to type.

So, the next time you feel it's appropriate to say thank you - do it with a handwritten note.

45 - Quickest Way To Begin
A Presentation

Every sales representative believes he's the master of sales presentations. There is a big difference between knowing some product attributes and being able to give a timely and professional sales presentation.

In medicine, doctors should not offer a prescription before they perform a physical exam. All too often, and usually within minutes of beginning a sales call, salespeople jump to premature product presentations. When this happens, here's what happens. You begin your sales presentation with insufficient customer information based on lots of assumptions. As you bungle your way through this presentation, if you're smart, you realize you're missing important pieces of information. Naturally, you start asking some questions.

From the potential customer's perspective he' s experiencing a discombobulated presentation that sets the stage for him to chime in and start asking about price. Defensiveness rears its ugly head once again and oftentimes we end up dueling with the prospect.

You might be wondering - is there a better and more efficient way to handle this situation? Yes, and indeed there is.

Let me suggest an appropriate and viable alternative. I believe every professional salesperson should have their own personalized selling model. Let me offer up the following as an example.

1. Identify qualified sales prospect.

2. Call to arrange first appointment.

3. Establish written sales call objectives.

4. Ask 8 to 12 prepared open-ended questions. (The number will depend on available time)

5. Use a prepared segue, bridge, or transition statement to set up your tailored presentation.

6. Proceed with your product presentation.

Isn't this a smoother and more professional approach from your customer's standpoint? When you complete your assessment of your prospects current situation the next logical step for you is to begin your presentation. Now, that's the good news - the bad news is, it can if you're not prepared, and create an awkward selling moment for you. To avoid this situation completely, consider using the following transition statement:

Remember you'll only use this when you've reached the point during the sales call when it's time to give your presentation.

Say this or something that's very similar:

"Based on what you've just told me" when you say this it says to your prospect - you have been listening.

Then say "I'd like to show you how XYZ (your company) will work with you on this project."

Now what this says is that you are about to deliver a very tailored presentation.

Two statements suggest two powerful things to your potential customer. They say you're listening and you're tailoring your presentation specifically for him. When you follow this model you end up saving time and creating a more favorable first impression with your potential customer.

46 – Get A Timer

The pace keeps getting quicker. There is one constant though - and that is, the time available always remains the same. We each have 24 hours or 1440 minutes to everyday. With all the daily distractions and interruptions it's easy to lose track of time. For example:

1. Telephone calls that you expect to take five minutes suddenly become 35 minutes if you don't pay attention.

2. If you're working in a branch office or a corporate office environment you're probably overwhelmed with meeting invitations. Everybody complains about going to too many meetings yet most people don't want to be left out of any.

3. Okay, so your "To Do" list is overwhelming, what can you do about it?

4. Special projects come up from time to time usually with plenty of notice. Your sales manager has asked you to prepare a two-hour presentation on pricing strategies for the next sales meeting scheduled in 60 days.

5. Big prospects usually demand big proposals and if you plan on personalizing it that can be time-consuming.

I can't change the work landscape for you, but I can make a suggestion that would allow you to have more control of your time enabling you to accomplish more in less time.

If you want more control over your time, you have to take time to monitor your *time* as your day progresses. Buy a timer. They work in two ways. You can set the timer for 15 minutes and as soon as you hit the start button your timer begins to countdown to zero. You can also set the timer to show elapsed time when you hit the start button.

For example, especially when you're making telephone calls from your office, time all telephone calls. Chances are if you're keeping track of the time your call will be more focused and definitely shorter.

Use a timer to keep track of meeting time. You'd be amazed at how much influence, power, and control you'd have when people in the meeting realized it was being timed.

For the special projects and things on your "To Do" list you can allocate specific chunks of time to tackle each item on your list.

The same is true for those big proposals. My advice is to set aside a block of time to work on the proposal and to keep track of that time with the timer. Most people lose track of the time. Timers on the other hand tend to keep you on track and on time.

It's easy to make time when you take the time to time what you are doing. Get a timer and use it!

47 - File It

Waiting time doesn't have to be wasted time. In fact, you can turn it into extremely productive time. Here's a tip that I have been doing for the last 25 years. If you're like me you don't like having somebody put you on hold forcing you to wait. You can turn this downtown time into productive time as soon as you buy 21 file folders.

This tip is extremely practical and necessary to achieving success in your sales career. By reading magazines and downloading articles from their websites you can build a reservoir of information that can help you through out your sales career. As you accumulate these articles put them in your reading file. The next time somebody keeps you waiting you can turn the waiting time into learning time.

I suggest you label these file folders in the following way:

Reading file - is where it all begins. First you read it then you file it. (This tip is important - that's why it's repeated)

Attitude - how you think is everything. Read everything you can to maintain your positive attitude.

Self-motivation - motivation is an inside job. Seek out very successful people as your role models to see how they stay motivated.

Goal setting - don't let your fear of failure hold you back. To learn all you can about goal setting read, read, and keep reading.

Time management - devour everything you can about this valuable subject.

Communication skills - learn how to balance your style with your substance.

Networking and prospecting - it's the beginning of every sales process. If you're not networking you're notworking.

Asking questions - is an art in the profession of selling. To achieve incredible success you must become an artist.

Analyzing behavioral styles - people are different. Learn what those differences are and how to adapt you're selling style to you buy is buying style.

Presentation skills - are essential to selling success. Discover how the pros do it.

Overcoming obstacles - these are the challenges you face on a daily basis. The good news is you get the same ones over and over again. Learn how the experts deal with these very same obstacles.

Securing commitment - is not as easy as most salespeople think it is. It's amazing how many salespeople don't know exactly how they will secure commitment for an order until they're sitting across the customer's desk.

Negotiating skills - are essential to your bottom line. You'd better step up and learn all you can about this topic.

Creativity - some people are more creative than others. Yet, everyone can learn how to become more creative than they are.

Listening - your ears will out earn your mouth every day of the week. Learn how to improve your listening skills.

Peak performance - discover what separates the winners from the whiners.

Pricing - every sale has a price. Every discounted dollar represents an equal loss in your revenue. Learn how to become a pricing Maestro.

Sales force automation - the automation landscape is changing daily. You have to keep up so you don't fall behind.

Telephone skills - it's an amazing tool. It's also amazing that so few people know how to properly use the telephone throughout the selling process.

Handling stress - is no laughing matter. The pace has never been quicker than it is today. We're surrounded by stress. Seek out ways that will help you to deal with the stresses in your life.

Value added selling - is essential to selling profitably. Do everything you can to become a master of explaining value throughout your selling process.

Trade shows - one thing is sure, if you're in sales sooner or later you'll get to work a trade show. Everything you ever wanted to know about tradeshow selling is in print.

Ultimately, you can save time by planning for your waiting time. Imagine the benefits that accrue to a salesperson that reads and keeps scores of information packed articles about the business of selling. Whenever you read an article written by a subject expert it's like putting him on your staff. If you ever need advice on that subject you now know where to find it.

48 - Avoiding Fire Drills

Sometimes during the sales training classes that I teach I'll do an exercise on the topic of time management. I divide the group into smaller mini groups of 3-5 Salespeople. It's usually a short five-minute exercise. I ask them to list all the distractions and interruptions they face on a daily basis.

Naturally the lists are usually the same. They include such things as the telephone, eMail, driving time, voice-mail, paperwork, customer requests, and management requests. Usually as we review these lists I see the look of quiet desperation on the faces in the audience. It's as though they have no control over such things.

The one thing however, I never hear, is the one thing that almost all salespeople do on a daily basis. When you're working with new prospects that offer large potential sales opportunities and when you're working with your biggest and best customers you want to show them how committed you are. One of the ways you're likely to demonstrate this commitment is to periodically ask the question "how soon do you need it?"

What a pathetic question! I'm serious, why in the world would you ever ask that question? I forgot, you want to show your commitment to serving your customers and newest prospects. What better way to do it than to ask the old and reliable question "how soon do you need it?"

Stop and think what kind of responses that question provokes. "I need it yesterday, ASAP, right away, immediately, today if possible, as soon as you can get it here." This is where the fire drill begins. You asked the question and you get their response and now the fire drill begins.

You reach for the phone to make your fast and furious telephone calls to the office. You beg, grovel, and plead your case with anyone who will listen. In fact, sometimes you drive everybody completely nuts. All because you asked the question "how soon do you need it?"

There is a better way. There is an alternative to asking this dreaded question and it will save you a bucket of time every day. Before you're tempted to ask "that question" go to your calendar to see when you are able to commit to completing the requested task. Once you have checked your calendar, you can then say to the customer "based on my schedule for the rest of the week I can get this information to you by Thursday morning 8 AM." You can also add at this point, "How does that work for you?"

I estimate 90 percent of the time your customers and prospects will be OK with what you just proposed. Now, you're only dealing with the fire drill 10 percent of the time and that should save you a considerable amount of time every day.

49 - Maintain Your Focus

Seven years ago I did a sales training program in Colorado. The meeting was held about two hours north of Denver, in a lodge situated in Roosevelt National Park. My client was, Low Alpine, a manufacturer of outdoor gear. Specifically, they made the stuff that Mt. Everest climbers would use to trek up that mountain.

My two-hour presentation was scheduled right after lunch. The speaker who preceded me before lunch, had an extremely interesting topic. He had a slide presentation showing his various attempts at climbing the incredible Mt. Everest. As you might imagine it was a powerful and extremely insightful presentation about the art and dangers of mountain climbing.

There were 25 salespeople at this meeting. Their climbing gear was sold to retailers. So they knew all about the climbing business. They also new, by reputation, many of the names the speaker referred to. Throughout his presentation everyone was glued to his seats with anticipation. He mixed his stories with slides, which was extremely effective.

Just before he ended his presentation he asked the group a question. He remarked, "There's a time when you're climbing, when you can almost feel depressed. You just feel low and down. Do you know when that is?"

My imagination started to run wild especially since the highest I ever climbed wasn't even climbing, it was an elevator ride to the top of the Empire State building. I thought surely the salespeople in the audience would know the answer to his question. They responded with things that I imagined; when you first begin the climb, when you only have 100 yards left, when you reach the top, and when you begin your descent. The speaker's body language and facial expression gave it all away - no one was close.

I was surprised by the answer - maybe you will be too. He said, "Climbers get down when bad weather sets in." He went on to explain that when bad weather sets in you can't see the peak - you lose sight of your goal and become easily distracted.

You might be wondering, what if anything does this have to do with time management? I see a very clear correlation. You see, like a mountain climber who can't see the peak, salespeople without clearly defined goals (daily, weekly, monthly, yearly) are more susceptible to daily interruptions and distractions, and more likely to waste their precious time resource.

You don't have to climb Mount Everest to appreciate how important keeping your eyes focused on your goals is to achieving the ultimate success in sales.

50 - Getting Hooked Up

Have you ever been to a hospital? There are two ways to get into a hospital. You can check in as a patient or visit the patient who has just checked in. If you have ever been in a hospital you have certainly seen the aluminum pole on wheels with the liquid in a bag attached - called an IV. IV refers to intra venous solutions. These IV bags usually contain medications and or nutrients to sustain the patient.

Enough about hospitals - I just wanted to make a connection with them. When you consider the very quick pace of today's sales environment it's easy to understand how salespeople become disconnected from the learning process. If you're interested in earning more, you'd better be interested in learning more. The difference between earning and learning is the letter "L" for love of knowledge.

This love of knowledge is not based on an attempt simply to "keep up." Keeping up won't differentiate you from your competition. A professional golfer once commented, "When you think you've got it, that's when you've had it." One of the best ways to acquire new knowledge about the selling profession is to imagine you're permanently hooked up to a selling IV.

The selling IV provides you with a continuous flow of new ideas that you can use in your daily selling environment.

Jim Meisenheimer

Your selling IV will provide you with information and knowledge from a variety of sources. For example:

Books on selling - you can explore the business section of any bookstore and/or visit Amazon.com and enter the keyword "selling."

Audiocassettes on selling - once again you can explore the business section of any bookstore and/or visit Amazon.com and enter the keyword "selling."

Sales related websites – including:

- Businessbyphone.com
- Salestrainingcamp.com
- Justsell.com
- Meisenheimer.com

Magazines on selling - including Selling Power and Sales and Marketing Management are two of the best.

Newspapers on selling - Investors Business Daily (IBD) has a Leaders and Success column daily which offers inspiration, information, motivation, and education on the subject of business and professional selling.

To be effective in your territory don't depend on binge learning. Binge learning usually occurs at your company's national sales meetings that often start at 7 AM and keep going until you drop at 11 PM. You do this for five days and you're supposed to be motivated and trained. Actually this process is brain draining.

There's a better way and it's to get hooked up to a selling IV as soon as you can. Make sure you maintain the connection. It's a more relaxed and more profitable way to learn as you grow in your territory.

Your sales manager will appreciate your effort and your customers will notice the difference.

Use this space to record your ideas:

51 - The Power Of Three

With so much technology available, I'm often amazed how little emphasis professional salespeople put on prospect/customer follow-ups. There's no better way to set yourself apart from your competition and at the same time show genuine interest in your customer/prospect by using appropriate and personalized follow-ups.

Here are three ways to follow-up on an initial meeting with a big prospect:

1. Within 12 hours of your initial meeting with your prospect send him an eMail. This eMail should be a thank you eMail. To make this effective begin with a thank you. Any thank you is appropriate except thanking somebody for his time. There are two reasons why you should avoid doing this. First, everybody does it. Second, your time is just as valuable as anyone else's. My guess is that he's not thanking you for your time.

The key to an effective thank you is in its specificity. Here are several examples:

"Thank you for giving me a plant/facilities tour."

"Thank you for introducing me to Bill Anderson, your vice president of engineering."

"Thank you for sharing your past and positive experiences in doing business with our company."

People will never tire of a thank you note/eMail as long as your note is very specific.

2. Within three days of your first meeting with this new prospect send him a hand written note. This handwritten note will arrive five to six days after your first meeting. Hopefully, you secured the follow-up appointment during your first visit. Your hand written note is an excellent way to confirm the second meeting date and time.

3. Within seven to 10 days after you first meeting send your prospect another hand written note attached to an article. This article should be a general-purpose business article that almost anyone could benefit from. For example, it could be an article on time management, new technology, or something related to your specific industry.

Send this article with a note that simply says, "FYI - thought you might be interested in seeing this" and sign your name.

These follow-ups add a nice touch to a very positive first impression. It shows genuine interest in your prospect. It shows some attention to detail. Because so few salespeople are this disciplined not only will it differentiate you, it will also enhance your professionalism from the prospects perspective.

Within 10 days you will accomplish the following - one meeting, one (thank you) email, one follow-up note card confirming your next appointment, and a note card attached to an informational article. Another way of looking at this - is it represents four different contacts with your new prospect. There are few risks when you follow this formula since very few salespeople invest the time and effort to nurture their new prospect relationships in this way.

If you want to add power and punch to your follow-ups, consider doing serial follow-ups. They will keep your name in front of your prospect, and undoubtedly have a positive and cumulative impact.

52 - Laminate Or Vegitate

During the act of selling, you use words to guide you through the selling process. So much of what you do is repetitive. Because it's repetitive you can make it brilliant with just a little preparation and practice. How come so many salespeople shun preparation and practice? The answer is plain and simple, salespeople honestly believe that being prepared and to a degree scripted, will make them "sound canned."

With a little preparation and practice you'll glide through your sales calls in less time. Do you think your sales calls will take more or less time once you have a better idea of what you'll say during the call? Logically, it stands to reason when you have your specific sales call objectives in writing and have scripted, yes I mean scripted key elements of the sales call, it's going to be a better and shorter sales call - for you and your potential customer. Let me give you several examples:

If you're in sales you probably have to arrange appointments in advance with a telephone call. To be an effective telephone call there should be some structure to it. It begins with a greeting, an introduction, and elevator speech, several qualifying questions, an attempt to link their problems with your solutions, and finally asking for a mutually convenient time to meet face-to-face. This is pretty straightforward and easily scripted. You can take out the "Ah's" and "Um's" and words like "I was wondering" and "I'm going to be in your area next week."

If you truly want to avoid sounding canned you have to prepare and practice what you want to say. Without preparation and a little practice you'll end up sounding like every other sales person in North America who improvises his telephone calls and presentations.

If you want to sound like everyone else - don't prepare. If you want to sound more professional and different from millions of ordinary salespeople you'd better prepare and practice what you're going to say before you begin saying it.

The easiest way to prepare is with pencil and paper, or fingers and keyboard whichever is more comfortable for you. Simply write the words that make you feel conversational and comfortable. For example, write the words next to the key elements below - remember these are the steps to securing an appointment using a telephone call

Greeting - (insert your greeting)

Your introduction - (insert your introduction)

Your elevator speech - (insert your elevator speech)

Several qualifying questions - (insert several questions - open ended preferably)

Link their problems with your solutions - (Our specialty is working with organizations - insert their problem)

Ask for the appointment - (insert exactly how you will ask for the appointment)

If you find this assignment difficult, imagine how good you're sounding to the customer when you're just winging it. If you have to stop and think about what you should be saying instead of knowing exactly what to say, it's an incredible opportunity for you to dress up key elements of your sales presentation. Here are several key elements that should also be scripted in order to increase your professionalism whenever you're talking with prospect/customers:

1. The questions you ask.

2. Key elements of your presentation.

3. How you handle the price objection.

4. How you ask for commitment.

5. How you ask for the follow-up appointment.

Here's my recommendation for making this radical concept work for you. Do one at time, for example, begin with the appointment telephone call. Write down what you're planning to say. Do some editing when you're finished. Set it aside for 24 hours. Read it out loud to hear how it sounds and to see how comfortable you are with the words you've chosen. Do some additional editing. Set it aside for another 24 hours and repeat this process until you're completely satisfied with your work.

Once you're satisfied retype what you have prepared in 16-point type. Take it to a print shop and ask that it be laminated. You now have a cue card. You can use your cue card to practice and to remind you what you should be saying when you making a telephone call to secure an appointment or when you're doing steps (1-5) above.

If it's worth saying it's worth laminating. If it's worth saying it's worth preparing and practicing before you begin talking with your prospect/customers. It takes time to save time and the time it takes to prepare these short scripts will in the long run save you a bundle of time. In addition to saving a bundle of time you will sound more professional because you won't be doing the "sales babble talk" that most of your competitors rely on because like most salespeople they confuse "sounding canned" with being prepared.

When you're prepared you don't have to think about what you're going to say, you can focus on how you're going to say it.

Use this space to record your ideas:

53 - Sandwiched Appointments

In the past it was easy to show up on a potential customer's doorstep and get a meeting without having a prearranged appointment. Today however, that's virtually impossible because people are so busy and overwhelmed in their jobs. When making appointments most salespeople arrange them with geography and time slots in mind.

For example, you ideally want to cluster your appointments within a close geographic proximity to each other - to minimize the drive time between sales calls. When setting appointments, most salespeople begin with the first appointment of the day and then try to fill the second appointment, the third appointment, the fourth appointment, etc.

In today's highly competitive sales environment your days can end up looking like a meandering river. With interruptions and distractions galore your selling days seldom go according to your original plan. It's easy to talk yourself out of making one more sales call, especially if it's been a tough day and especially if it's the end of the day.

Here's a tip from Tony Puchowski with Curtis 1000. Tony has a novel approach when setting up his daily appointments. The first two appointments he confirms are for 8 a.m. and 4 p.m. This creates a psychological advantage for Tony that has the additional benefit of having a positive impact on his selling results. Tony figures it forces him to get out in the field early and creates a self-discipline that allows him to work a full day every day.

This minor adjustment or sandwiched approach to setting appointments gets Tony motivated and allows him to be more effective on a daily basis. It's a small tip that will pay big dividends for you.

54 - Measure Twice, Cut Once

Have you ever worried that putting together a plan will take too much time? Well not having a plan takes even more time! Why? Without a sales plan it's easy to get distracted from your goals increasing the probability that what's important may not get done.

There's something elusive about sales planning for professional salespeople. It's almost like taking medicine that you know isn't going to taste good. You know that it's going to be good for you, yet you keep putting off the decision to take it.

Occasionally, during my sales training programs I do an exercise in sales planning. This exercise is so simple to do, most salespeople fail miserably at doing it. Using a PowerPoint slide, I tell salespeople they are about to make a first sales call to a big prospect. The assignment is simply to write down their objectives for the sales call.

You're thinking, "What could be easier?" I have literally asked thousands of salespeople to perform this small yet important task. Common responses include:

≡ The purpose of this call is to introduce myself.

≡ The purpose of this call is to build rapport.

≡ The purpose of this call is to determine customer needs.

≡ The purpose of this call is to get an order.

≡ The purpose of this call is to tell the prospect our products/services can help him.

≡ The purpose of this call is to set up the second meeting.

And the list goes on. This is not complicated exercise because it only takes to a few minutes to complete. As salespeople are doing the exercise I walk around the room, peering over shoulders trying to identify three volunteers. Actually, I could ask anyone in the room to volunteer - since most people have the same fatal flaw in pre-call planning.

I ask each of the three volunteers to read their objectives to the audience. Then, I ask the three volunteers to follow me outside the room and help them to transform their objectives in less then three minutes.

What makes planning so important to selling is its influence on the direction and outcome of every sales call. You see, what most pre-call objectives have in common is the lack of specificity. First, a majority of salespeople don't take the time to prepare and write the sales call objectives before the call. Second, most sales call objectives are not quantifiable.

Here is an example of how to make general objectives more specific:

≡ The purpose of this call is to determine customer needs by asking 3-5 open-ended questions.

≡ The purpose of this call is to secure an order of at least $1250.

≡ The purpose of this call is to set up the second meeting within (3) weeks.

A simple number converts a general objective into a more specific one. With intelligent planning and effective execution salespeople can radically improve their selling numbers. Here are three plans that should always be in writing:

1. Pre-call objectives. Think of it as a flight plan for your sales call.

2. Post call plans. An effective start-up requires the appropriate follow-up.

3. Account plans. You'll achieve more when you commit in writing to what you want to achieve. Also note when you want to get it done in your key accounts.

To summarize, there are two keys to effective planning. First and foremost your plan must be in writing. You then have to check your plans to make sure they are quantifiable and measurable. If you can measure it you can do it, if you can't you won't.

If you measure twice you can probably cut once. There's a reason this is an old saying. The simple reason is - it works. You will see an immediate and noticeable difference in your selling results when you plan it, then do it.

What's the one thing you've learned about planning?

55 - Got To Go

Got to go - the art of ending a sales call. Plain and simple most salespeople have never given sufficient thought and/or planning on how to end a routine sales call.

Usually, the cue is customer driven. It begins with a peek at a watch, a little restlessness, or even a comment about having to go to a 2 p.m. meeting. In any case, the salesperson obliges, if he's attentive, and takes this signal to move on to the next sales call.

Just before leaving you might even utter this pathetic phrase, "Before I go are there any other problems I can help you with?"

Granted - ending a sales call is no big thing or is it? Do you really have any options on how you end your sales call? Sure you do:

1. You can just fade away.

2. You can disappear quickly.

3. You can pleasantly say goodbye.

4. You can (imagine this) try to up-sell and/or cross-sell some of your products/services.

Imagine telling your spouse you're going to the supermarket and asking, "Do you need anything?" It's probably 50/50 whether or not your spouse adds something to your shopping list.

Imagine doing this in a slightly different matter. What if you told your spouse you're going to the supermarket and said, "I'll be walking past the meat market, the fish market, produce, soups, coffee, cereal, fresh flowers, liquor, pharmacy, and cosmetics - do you need anything?"

Now, what's the probability you'll trigger a need and get a response? You'll have to agree it's much higher.

How many times after you leave a customer's office do you think they remember something they needed but forgot while you were there? It happens more than you want to know.

My recommendation for the perfect segue to your departure is for you to slowly take them on a mental tour of your product offering to see if there's anything else you can help them with before you go.

Your customers will appreciate your thoughtfulness and you'll appreciate getting the extra business.

Part IV

Managing The Miscellaneous

56 – Now What

Lord Chesterfield once said, "Know the true value of time; snatch, seize, and enjoy every moment of it. No idleness, no delay, no procrastination; never put off till tomorrow what you can do today.

Here are three questions to ponder as you begin to take more control of your time and your life.

1. What can you start doing immediately?

2. What can you stop doing immediately?

3. What can you change immediately?

You don't need permission to get started. **Just do it**!

57– Timing Is Everything – Words Of Wisdom

A moment's insight is sometimes worth a life's experience.
O.W. Holmes

Time is the scarcest resource and unless it is managed,
nothing else can be managed. Peter Drucker

Spilled water never returns to the cup. Japanese Proverb

No pessimist ever won a battle.
Dwight Eisenhower

You work hard and you're finally on Easy Street; then you
discover there's no parking. Anonymous

The bold are helpless without cleverness. Euripides

You may be disappointed if you fail, but you are doomed if
you don't try.
Beverly Sills

The time,which we have at our disposal every day is
elastic; the passions that we feel expand it; those that we
inspire contract it; and habit fills up what remains.
Anonymous

57 Ways To Take Control Of Your Time And Your Life

Why kill time when one can employ it?
French proverb

The only person to succeed while horsing around is a
bookie. Bob Murphy

Yesterday is a cancelled check. Tomorrow is a promissory
note. Today is cash in hand; spend it wisely. Kay Lyons

Don't lose your head to gain a minute. You need your
head. Your brains are in it. Burma Shave Ad

It is not enough to aim. You must hit. Harry Truman

The road to success runs uphill; so don't expect to break
any speed records. Anonymous

Consider the postage stamp: its usefulness consists in the
ability to stick to one thing till it gets there. Josh Billings

The ultimate inspiration is the deadline. Nolan Bushnell

Talk does not cook rice. Chinese Proverb

A good beginning makes a good ending.   English Proverb

Don't mistake activity for achievement. John Wooden

Empty pockets never held anyone back. Only empty heads
and empty hearts can do that. Norman Vincent Peale

We all find time to do what we really want to do.
William Feather

Do nothing, and nothing happens. Do something, and something happens.
Benjamin Franklin

It's a job that's never started that takes the longest to do.
Tolkien

What is the use of running when we are not on the right road? German Proverb

Work only half a day. It makes no difference which half the first 12 hours or the last. Kemmons Wilson

Tomorrow is often the busiest day of the week.
Anonymous

Ignorance is not bliss. It's oblivion. Phillip Wylie

You don't get to choose how you're going to die or when. You can only decide how you're going to live now.
Joan Baez

Don't tell me how hard you work. Tell me how much you get done. James Ling

Don't measure yourself by what you've accomplished, but rather by what you should have accomplished with your abilities. John Wooden

Execution is the chariot of genius.
William Blake

It is never too late to be what you might have been.
George Eliot

Talking is a disease of age.
Ben Johnson

We talk little, if we do not talk about ourselves.
William Hazlitt

The four-letter word for psychotherapy is talk.
Eric Hodgins

It isn't that they can't see the solution. It is that they can't
see the problem.
G.K. Chesterton

Beware the fury of a patient man.
John Dryden

Jim Meisenheimer Client Services

* First and foremost a "Sales Strategist"

* Corporate consulting - includes strategic planning

* Keynote speaking

* Results oriented sales development programs

* Assessment tools for hiring

* Selling Systems - books, tapes, white papers

* Personal coaching for senior executives

* Personal coaching for professional salespeople

* Monthly TeleSeminars

* Advanced Sales Management Workshops

* Advanced Sales Boot Camps

* Website: http://www.meisenheimer.com

About Jim Meisenheimer

Jim Meisenheimer was born in New York City and was raised in West Babylon Long Island. He graduated from the University of Rhode Island and did graduate work at St. Johns University.

He is a former U.S. army officer serving in Germany and was a Public Information Officer on a General's Staff while serving in Vietnam. He was also Vice President of Sales and Marketing for the Scientific Products Division of Baxter International. His other responsibilities included sales representative, regional sales manager, marketing manager, Director of Marketing, and Vice President Sales and Vice President of Marketing.

He has earned the designation CSP (Certified Speaking Professional) from the National Speakers Association. He is a charter member of Master Speakers International. He has authored five books including the recently published "57 Ways To Take Control Of Your Time And Your Life."

He has worked with 417 different organizations. Last year 68% of his business was repeat business.

His clients include: Abbott, Baxter, Alcoa, Allstate, Bell & Howell, AmerisourceBergen, Briggs and Stratton, Canadian Airlines, Caterpillar, Corning, Kodak, Ericsson, Fanniemae, General Motors, Hewlett-Packard, Johns HopkinsUniversity, Kraft, Loyola University, Northern Trust, Novartis, Pinkerton, U.S. Healthcare, U.S. Borax, U.S. Postal Service, Xerox, and Zenith Electronics.

Jim Meisenheimer, Inc. has achieved 15 consecutive years of increased sales and profitability.

Jim Meisenheimer

FAX Order Form 847-680-7881

Item	Price	No.	Total

Books

47 Ways to Sell Smarter	$19.95		
50 More Ways To Sell Smarter	$19.95		
How To Double Your Sales			
Without Quadrupling Your Effort	$19.95		
The Twelve Best Questions To Ask Customers	$19.95		
57 Ways To Take Control Of Your Time And Your Life	$19.95		

Audio Cassettes

How To Get Surefire Selling Results (Tapes or CD's)	$199.00		
How To Win More Sales	$19.95		
The Twelve Best Questions To Ask Customers	$19.95		
Maximum Results In Minimum Time	$19.95		
How To Double Your Business			
Without Quadrupling Your Effort	$19.95		
Closing the Sale	$19.95		

Special Recordings

#1 – Advanced Sales Management Course (16 CD's)	$397.00		
#2 – How To Sell Anything for List Price	$57.00		
#3 – Eight Ways To Outfox The Competition	$57.00		

Individual Assessments

Personal Insights Profile – DISC	$20.00		
	Subtotal		
Tax (FL residents add 6.5%)			
Shipping & handling: $5.00 in U.S. – International will be added			
	TOTAL		

Please call for special value pricing when ordering large quantities.

Method of Payment: Check or money order payable to Jim Meisenheimer, Inc:
Credit Card: ❑ Visa ❑ Master Card ❑ Amex

No:_____ Exp. Date:_____
Name:_____ Company_____
Street Address_____ City/State/Zip_____
Phone_____ FAX_____ eMail_____